THESE THOUSANDS OF DAYS

Aaron Childress

THESE THOUSANDS OF DAYS

This is What I Learned After I Killed Myself

Published by CL Publishing.
626 S. Tyler Rd. #75161
Wichita, Kansas 67275

Printed in the United States of America
ISBN: 9798375814018 (hardcover)
ISBN: 9798375704708 (paperback)
Library of Congress Control Number: 2023902134

Names: Childress, Aaron, author.
Title: These thousands of days : this is what I learned after I killed myself /
        Aaron Childress.
Description: Wichita, Kansas : Childress Limited, [2023]
Identifiers: ISBN: 9798375814018 (hardcover) | 9798375704708 (paperback)
Subjects: LCSH: Suicidal behavior. | Mental health. | Mind and body
        therapies. | Emotions--Health aspects. | Meditation--Health
        aspects. | Mindfulness (Psychology)--Health aspects. | Emotional
        intelligence. | Emotion recognition--Health aspects. | Self-
        consciousness (Awareness) | Post-traumatic stress disorder--
        Alternative treatment. | Psychic trauma-- Alternative treatment. |
        Stress management--Alternative treatment. | Change
        (Psychology) | LCGFT: Self-help publications.
Classification: LCC: RC569 .C45 2023 | DDC: 616.85/8445--dc23

Cover art, book, and digital design by Aaron Childress

CONTENTS

INTRODUCTION

I've wanted to write this for a while, but because I let circumstances derail me, I have just now found my way around completing it. The unintended benefit of that is because of my wandering off the path; I often found myself immersed in various methods and disciplines, studying my mind and how it works. I didn't write this at the beginning of my journey. However, it was tempting to do so. You will learn from my journey, mostly through storytelling with splashes of poetry. This is not intended to be a textbook but stories and lessons.

I gained experience as a television host, which made me comfortable in front of audiences. That propelled me to do keynote speeches, teaching me to structure topics and engage people face-to-face. From there, I transitioned into public relations, where I learned about other people's emotions during their highs and lows. After working in public relations, I moved into sales, where I combined emotional intelligence with what I say to become an effective salesperson. This combination of skills helped me achieve a worthwhile goal for both the customer and me. This writing developed through the application of all these tools.

Some people love lengthy books. I don't. I wanted both the text and the audio versions of this writing to be something that can be read or listened to in one sitting. Furthermore, though this is written for you, it also serves as a journal entry to myself since I am still training my mind. I will never stop that pursuit. It would be best if you never stopped that pursuit either.

Part of this pursuit is the belief that if I can explain these principles to a child, then I truly understand them. More writings will follow this one in the hope that each writing will become simpler. My strict belief in this process is built on the idea that if something is genuinely positive for me or helpful for others, it shouldn't be reserved for those with an extensive vocabulary. Children suffer too, so my goal is to eventually be so well-versed in explaining the principles in this writing that I can convey them to children and young adults.

I first had this notion when I watched someone explain scripture from the Bible while using large words and incredible effort to sound brilliant. It struck me as odd because if the message was unifying and life-defining, why was it only spoken to people with a collegiate-level understanding? Though I have a degree, ordination, and a few other things along the way, my goal is to explain these things to everyone. Not just those who understand large words. It's unfair to have this knowledge and keep it for only those who can serve my ego. This knowledge is for everyone. No exceptions. So, I hope to keep this as simple as possible, and each writing beyond this be even more straightforward.

The simple secret is that I already know the last message I will write. However, I still need to build the framework to write it, even though I see it, albeit in the dimly lit mirror ahead of me. I must keep that message to myself until then because the final text is not the goal; the journey is. I know that's the cliché part of these writings about your mind, but it's the painful truth that part of this process is wanting to be on this path. You'll be unable to access it properly if you're told everything all at once. It will be like a seed thrown on the rocks.

CHAPTER 1

With No Timidity

I am not writing to you in any timidity, nor am I writing to you as one of many. I am writing to you as one of the few who survived the drop. That is not an honor. However, I am writing you as one of the even fewer who survived beyond the aftermath of the drop. Almost none of us exist; we are very few. Also, I am among the few who carried the healing past worldly doctrines into the truth and hope, into the path beyond self. I cannot have this path and not speak about it. What I am saying will produce fruit: immeasurably. I will not back down from the hope within this message.

I am writing this to share my journey, earlier suffering, and the principles that have helped me become who and what I am today. But more importantly, it is time for you to embark on your journey of self-discovery and healing. This journey will be challenging and will not happen in one day. It is time to address this all now.

However, it is unfortunate that for some, it is too late. I am tired of being too late. I am no longer too late. I start this part of my journey to prevent others from finding my same fate.

In this writing, you will learn about my journey, the principles that led me to where I am today, and about yourself. You will discover how your mind, emotions, and body work together as a team, with you as the leader. I will also provide techniques to aid in becoming a better manager of yourself.

You will become a better manager of yourself, which in turn will improve your ability to handle others. I have suffered in the past, but I have survived and become stronger.

The lessons I have learned are valuable, and I want to pass them on to you. My aim is not to focus on the negative aspects of life but to promote completeness and wholeness.

These teachings are not secrets but are misconceptions and things covered up - words buried for days, uncovered by the willing few. I, too, held these misconceptions until I decided to stop letting my mind deceive me.

To discover these teachings, you must change how you treat yourself and others. My ultimate goal is not just to help those who suffer from thoughts of suicide but to help all people who suffer from any attack from their minds. This message mentions a few suicides, including mine; however, this writing is not solely about suicide. It is about self-discovery and growth.

I found the cure when I entered. Before I entered, I was still susceptible to "the demons" lurking in my mind. They have no power now. Until you enter, they are strong. So, do not be submissive to them, and do not lie to yourself and think the paths of the masses solve them. They do not. The masses design the ways of the masses to keep you. But they may mend you for a time. Recognize them for what they are, take all thoughts captive, but continue this path.

You will be alone on this journey, as I was. That is the way. Soon, you will feel even more alone. Then you will discover that you were never alone. But if you take someone with you for comfort, you both will stay alone.

So, travel alone until you find that you were never alone. And that discovery will be the day you meet you. Something even more incredible than you and I will be there that day. Though it will be greater, you and I will be in it. And it in you and I. Immeasurable.

I want to address the "seek help" notion briefly. I did not reach my current state of well-being alone at first. Even though I just said you must travel alone. Before I found the way, my only choice was to seek help from medical doctors, psychologists, psychiatrists, pastors, and counselors. Albeit inadvertently, they were the ones who started me on this path.

I found that often and almost always, their help did not go far enough. Their support came to the door, but that door, too often, was a lifetime prescription or a quote meant to drive emotion. I didn't want medicine or emotion that would keep me bound for life. I wanted freedom, a cure.

This message is intended to be a nudge to encourage you to seek. If someone brought you to the door, thank them, and then move forward alone. It is okay for someone to nudge you to this path, but to enter, you must eventually decide that it is worth it even as you go it alone. You must go it alone. No one can take you inside. I cannot take you inside. I can only bring you to the door. You must enter.

This message is a story about self-discovery and the realization that you play a role in your well-being. It is essential to be mindful of your mental health and cautious when seeking help.

While there are many great people in the mental health profession, some individuals may only help for their benefit, and some employ practices that have been around for decades with little to no success.

I have chosen ancient ways, as modern thought and man's doctrines have removed the search for the true self. Man's doctrines allow you to define yourself with attachments. I opened the door and entered.

I am healed and cured of my suffering. I have peace. I know who and what I am. That does not mean that I never see attacks. I see them for what they are, and they have no power. But they still try. The attacks from any perspective and in any direction of your unfocused eye will not stop. But when you know yourself, you know others, and the attacks do not bring about the anger they are looking for. The attacks find that you are at peace, which becomes an unintended attack on them. Peace angers people.

One last item, if you are approaching this from a concept of faith, yes, these topics will sometimes feel like you are explaining away God or even replacing yourself as God. Do not stress. That is not what is happening. And that is not the intent.

It appears that way because the values you hold dear are trying to regain their place. Your doctrines, and man's doctrines, are trying to push away any threats to the status quo.

I came to this crossroads very early on. But this thought might help you at that moment: If God is real, and He is the creator, there should not be a limit placed on Him by you or me. If someone could quickly explain God to me, that is not the god I wanted to follow.

I wanted the God that I could not explain with quotes and small talk; I wanted to know the mystery. I felt that a god who man could describe in detail was a product of man. That was man's doctrine. If you want a god who man can describe with human words, that is your choice.

I chose early on that if I was going to believe in God, I had better run at Him without worrying about the limits of man's doctrine. You will find many troubling truths as you begin to heal. You will be upset to discover that you believe you are more like a god than you ever knew. By the end, you will be closer to the truth.

Not only will you find that you are not God, but you may also discover a new view to aid you in your pursuit of God. You will heal your ego and come down from your elevated sense of self to find who and what you are. And while who and what you are is more magnificent than I have words to describe, you are also part of the whole. And when you find that you are part of the whole, you become whole.

But you will not be whole while believing you are the whole. You are not God. Do not think I will tell you to claim that. And do not think that I will tell you that He does not exist either.

With that being said, this is not a writing of faith. It is a story about overcoming intense personal suffering to find peace and wholeness. The practices can be used to expand your faith or other areas that do not include any faith principles. I incorporate faith principles in my life, but you might not. With that in mind, this story is for all people who have met the same demons as me.

You will know when you enter because humility is there. Peace is there. But the practices within this message can, unfortunately, be used by those who look to manipulate you. Those who use these practices for insidious purposes cannot find peace or humility.

They are counterfeits. They will employ these same works to manipulate and strangle. When they got to the new door, they chose their current state instead of entering and reentered from which door they came. They used this as an attachment for gain.

Know them because while they too may speak with authority, they seek their own needs without peace and in no humility. They do not want you to find the door. They will hide it from you. Because in that door, they have no power. Know them by their lack of compassion, humility, and desire to obstruct peace. You will know them by their lack of control of even positive emotions. Continue the path: wholeness, peace, and humility.

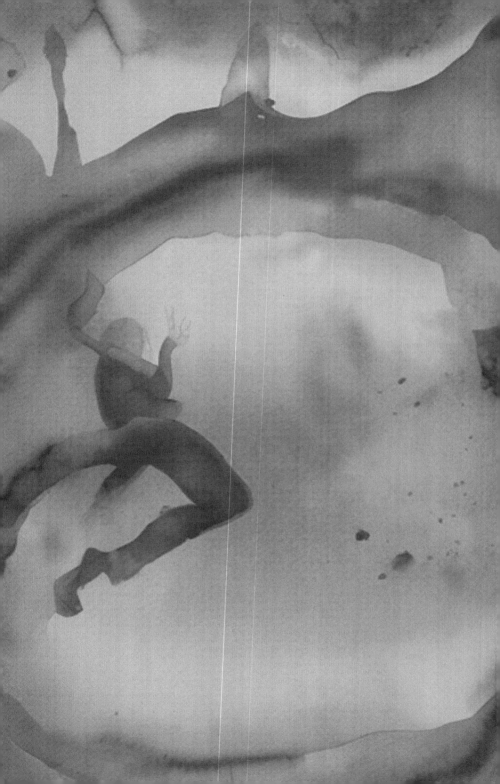

THE CYCLE

For most of my life, I have been researching my mind in the physical and beyond. I was diagnosed with epilepsy in my early twenties. It's a rare type that degenerated my motor skills over time, and there weren't many options. This form subjected me to dozens of seizures a day. Most of them were small, some large. The treatment options for this epilepsy were like a prison. So, I chose to live with it. That's where this whole process began.

I tried various forms of medication over the years. Still, I found that sobriety on medication was far better than being chained to pills and side effects. Neither of which cures but instead adds another permanent layer of dependency. I found that any synthetic entry into my body hindered this process. However, your journey is your own, and you should make the choices that suit your needs if medicinal abstinence doesn't work for you.

As I abstained from medication as best I could, I found myself on a path to finding a cure for my epilepsy. And in this search, I met myself. I met my mind and was introduced to my thoughts, reason, and emotions: me. I found the answer to the question: "Who and what am I?"

I entered this state a few years ago after this study became a hyper-focused survival tool.

Breaking through all this was a charge that altered my spectrum. Even more profoundly than the rope of a degenerating brain. I made a choice. I made a split-second decision that rippled the particles forward and backward in time and settled into this eternity. I built my prison: the cycle.

I am reminded of a story I once heard many years ago. It was about a news reporter covering a national event. The main character in this story was a man much like I used to be. This man was selfish, inconsiderate, and always chose his own needs over others. He often went out of his way to hurt others without a second thought.

But as the cycle story unfolds, something strange happens to this man. He wakes up on what he believes is the next day, only to realize that it is not the next day. It is the same day that he just went through, with the only deviation being his actions or the actions of those he directly affects.

He realizes that he is the main focal point of this cycle and that the cycle has chosen him against his will. At first, he is confused by this repetition. His self-serving nature only deepens, and he becomes worse, learning tricks to manipulate others and using the cycle as a weapon. But as time passes, the amusement wears off, and the dread of this personal prison sets in. He cannot find a way out of this madness.

But then, one day, something clicks. He realizes that he has been missing the whole point of the cycle. He realizes that the cycle is not an accident but a message to him. He has been chosen by the cycle because he is causing pain in others and needs to be stopped. Instead of just killing him, the cycle has set him in this personal prison. It seems to be a form of grace for both the victims of his ego and himself. The message is clear: he must make a change. He must learn to find the compassion to move past the repetition and the personal prison.

I was bullied as a kid, then suffered loss while in the Marines. I was in my mid-thirties, had just lost my dream job, and my family was hurting. I became selfish, causing pain to those around me. Then, I, too, found myself stuck in a cycle and could not break free. Every day cycled for me like a personal hell. Many parallels between the main character and myself strike me.

As I reflected, I realized it was time for me to change, find the compassion to move past my ego, and start considering the needs of others. I am cured and whole. Now I want to show you that journey from start to finish. In all of this, I hope you realize it is time for you to find this path.

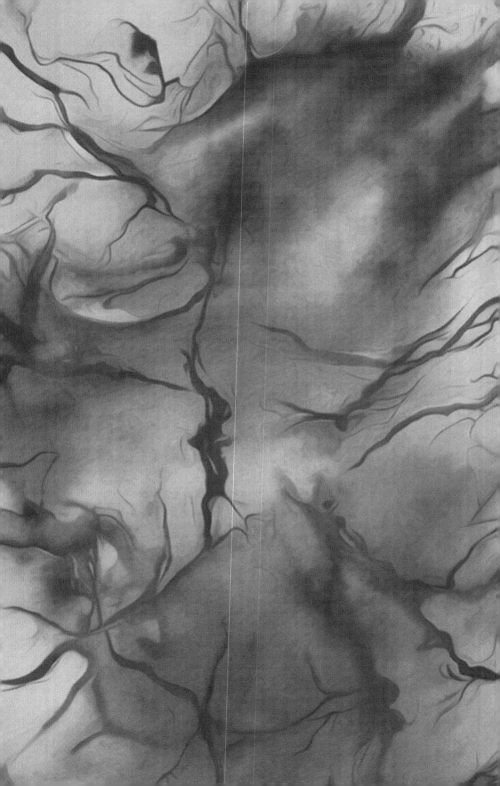

CHAPTER 2

The Worldly Grief

To begin this journey, I need to share a story that almost derailed everything before it could truly start. This story is not the beginning but rather the result of various misconceptions I had about myself. I want you to take a moment and visualize me in a calm state. I am sitting comfortably in a recliner, with my feet kicked up with a screen in front of me. I am relaxed and at peace.

However, something suddenly takes over me without warning, and my mood changes instantly. This shift is intense and swift, altering my entire demeanor. The calmness I once felt is replaced by a wave of intense emotions that leave me overwhelmed and off balance. This is an uneasy story that I must share, as it is crucial to understanding my journey and the challenges I have faced along the way.

Can You Come Get Me?

There comes a time when you realize,
You are too young to be good at final goodbyes.
There is a power without definition.
A gentle greeting from a friend,
But no face to see.
Just a simple gesture of kindness,
Despite the fingers crossed behind his back.
Every step along the way builds up inside you,
And all you feel is the emptiness of memories.

Memories seem to hold so much weight at first glance,
But they carry only a foul wind.
They used to comfort me,
They would fade into my thoughts,
Life was good.
You choked the good days, friend.
Removed them from my mind.
I'm no longer reminded of the good days.
The daydreams have grown into weeds.

So, I sit here quietly with you.
We watch the weeds grow.
Here in the quiet calm.
Watching the sky turn black.
Behind those growing tares.
Ominous.

Arms tremor slightly with each pump of my heart.
The tremor flows in my veins, through my arms.
An eerie calm pours over my body in the room.
There is a cold wind; hair stands on the alarm.
Pressure mounts, but the calm still holds me.
I feel you, but I can't I see you with me?
My teeth are grinding, jaw tightening.
My breath stuttering, lungs igniting.
My legs tighten, forced to stand.
My eyes clouding, rigid hands.
I take one step, and one more.
Another one, three, then four.
The air has become electric.
Please tell me your name.
Lean into the momentum.
Pull the restraints away.
This is darker than fear.
The door swings wide.
Do I want to do this?
Please, reach inside.
Can you stop me?
Please just reach!
Pace is growing!
Gathering ease.
One more step!
On the ladder!
To the top!
Last step!
Rope!

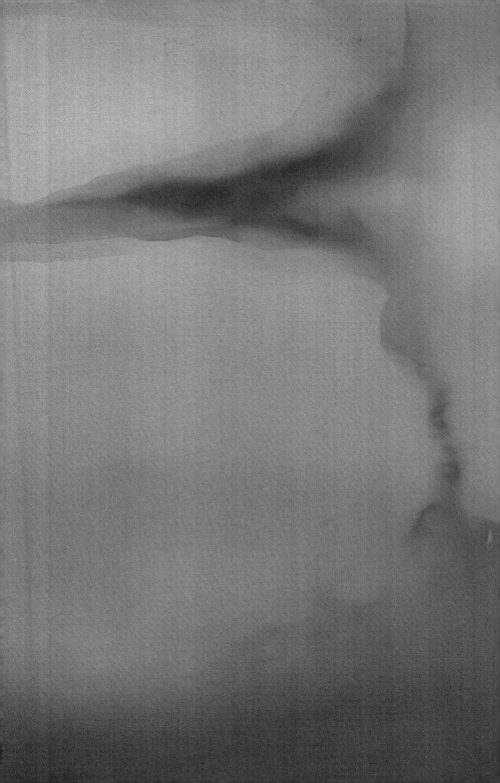

drop.

The light fades.
The corners of my eyes blur.
The white wisps begin to flutter.
White flashes through the blackening.
My face is on fire, but no smoke in my lungs.
That pressure, crushing pressure, will be over soon.

Please. Just. Get. Past. This. Last. Moment. Every
breaker switch is being tripped. I waited for that main
switch. My final goodbye to it all. My last lights to go
out. One by one. I'm drowning, but I'm on dry land.

A blur forms through a light.
A black figure in front of me rushes.
Is it you who wouldn't tell me your name?
This is the one who shuts the final breaker.
The final light. The worldly grief that produces death. It
rushes me, that dull impact, a crushing grasp, A dark
shadow, The owner of death. At last. A jet engine howl
erupts in my ears. Beyond that howl is the cry.
I can't find my breath.
I beat pain.
I beat it.
I won.

Mom?
Can you come get me?
I was too young to be good at final goodbyes.

SEEING BEYOND THIS STAGE

I heard that cry through the howl, "Please don't do this!" it cried. That ringing in my ears wouldn't stop, and everything was muffled behind it. I heard yelling, I heard crying, and I heard the voice come into the clear from the deep. It repeated, "You can't do this! I'm not letting you do this!"

I opened my eyes and found myself watching this all play out. Everything was hazy and indistinct, like a dream. I looked around and saw my wife holding my waist, head down, and crying. I was detached and confused. I tried to move but couldn't feel my body because I felt lighter than air - zero gravity with no pain. This had to be death. I couldn't tell if I was breathing.

I remembered coming out here. I remember the electricity. I remembered the drop. Everything after that was a blur. I must have done it. I tried to speak, but no sound came out. I was like a fish out of water, invisible and unheard. I felt a deep sadness and despair. I couldn't believe that I had done it. It felt different than I expected. I didn't leave my prison. I found a new one. I think I put her in one too.

My wife was able to get me down from the noose. I was immediately checked into the hospital for a medical and mental evaluation. We were both stunned, shocked, and confused. We said no words to each other in the hours after it happened. We had broken the fourth wall of our minds because the shock and adrenaline were crashing our brains so hard that we could not stay inside our heads. We were looking out into the audience of hope waiting for us to speak. But we couldn't speak.

On top of that, I had physical effects with which I was dealing. The air went silent for weeks. Blank stares across the room, blank lines on the script, and blank hearts became overgrown with so many emotions that the crowd of pain was the steady ring of a flatline – almost soothing, yet, terrifying. Two people, both dead.

It had been a few weeks since I opened my eyes to this world again. I heard that cry and the howl constantly. I wasn't happy that I couldn't complete that job, and I didn't feel any different. I might have even felt worse, not because I did it, but because I couldn't do it. People gave me sympathy as though I was happy about the outcome. I wasn't even sure what the outcome actually was.

I couldn't even tell if I was alive. Every day was a cycle: was this hell? I ended up stuck in this chasm between the living and the dead. Did I actually survive? Cycling over these thousands of days made me think that maybe I didn't survive.

THE BRAZEN AUDACITY TO WIN

I found myself sitting in a room. I was stuck and still full of failure. I spent some time at home recuperating and some of my time in facilities. My first breakthrough happened on a visit to a mental health facility where I was being monitored for possible relapse.

During one particular daily mental health checkup with the psychiatrist assigned to me, the doctor mentioned that he, too, would go to a psychiatrist regularly. He threw that comment out to me nonchalantly while scribbling on his notepad. This blew my mind! He was supposed to be fixing me, but he needed fixing!?

At first, I was a bit unnerved by this, and I stopped him from scribbling. He elaborated on his process, saying, "I hear everybody's worst day, every day. That stuff has to go somewhere. I see people at their worst moments in life and some of the worst situations. I see it, and it has to go somewhere. It can't stay inside of me and grow."

He talked about how he grew up in a country that was always in civil war, so he had been dealing with the darkest scenes on earth his entire life.

This man changed my whole direction of focus in one conversation, and he wasn't even technically helping me at that moment.

He was telling a fact about his life. I was sitting in a white room, sulking about my worries. Then, it occurred to me. This man was fighting for people, and because of that, he needed to talk to someone else about what was going on in his life. I had been holding on to things and letting them live in my mind. I didn't know I could ever remove these movies in my mind.

Before this, I wouldn't have agreed to any form of counseling. I saw it as a sign of weakness. I saw doctors as people who pushed unending prescriptions instead of trying to help people because their job security relied on sick patients, not cured patients. But when I changed my view from macro to micro, I saw the man in front of me. Even though I had an aversion to this type of therapy, I saw past that and into something that could help me.

I'm not saying that my fears of that industry are not founded on principles that counter mine. It didn't matter at that moment because I met a compassionate person who wanted to save my life. I didn't need him to solve the journey. I only needed one step. He gave me the first step to saving my life. I was still dead before that moment. He knew it. I knew it. The next moment knew it. When the path ahead looked grim, He had the brazen audacity to win.

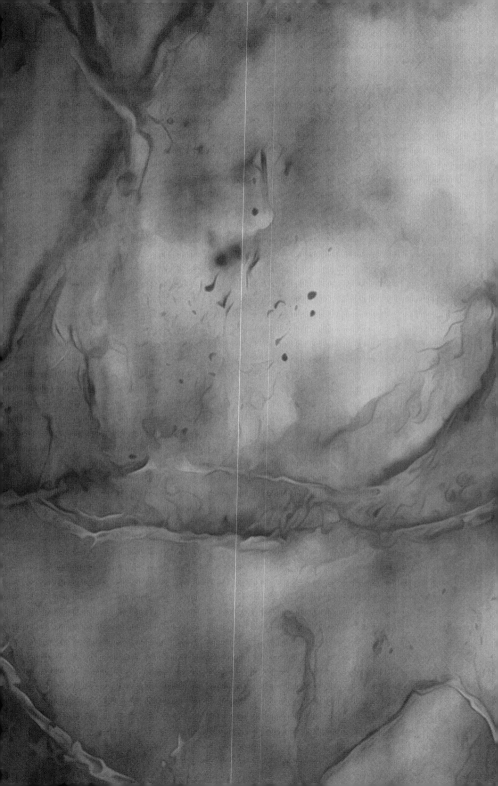

CHAPTER 3

The Ineffable

The quick definition of "ineffable" is that something is so profound that I cannot use language to describe it. You may say the word "awesome" is in this same spectrum. However, the definition of "awesome" is that something inspires awe and wonder. You could look at something, stare at it with your mouth gaping, and say, "wow." That is "awe." That is awesome.

Ineffable is beyond that. I would go so far as to say defining "ineffable" is a paradox. Because if ineffable is without definition, then even the meaning and word should not exist.

So, what happened? What did I do? What do I know now that I didn't know then? After committing this act, I began medical and mental rehabilitation, hoping that we could find the cause of my urge to kill myself.

The doctor seems to think physical activity will help relieve stress. So, I went swimming in a pool, but my thoughts were floating in my mind. I went to the gym and played basketball, but I'm not uncovering anything beyond a temporary lift in my emotions. Nothing is working.

What did I do? I still want to do it again. Did you notice anything? You came here for that part of the story, right? What did you see? Did anything stand out that may be different from what you expected? Let me add one ingredient to the mix that may change your perception of the scene.

I wasn't depressed. I was fine. At least I was right up until the moment before the drop. I was sitting in a room in my recliner with my feet kicked up. I am relaxing, looking at the screen in front of me.

I was calm in that moment. I was a deeply depressed person who had been battling depression for a long time. But at that moment, I was not in actual depression. I was upbeat.

This thought was alarming because suicide and depression go hand-in-hand, don't they? Well, they do, but you have to look closer.

What I soon discovered was that my suicide did not happen that day. It was a series of events. Let's dissect my mind. You have me. You have my mind. I'm here. So, let's take this opportunity to dissect me.

CHARLATANS OF HOPE

The ineffable nature of the emotion which occurs during suicide is stronger than a phone call. It's stronger than the love for a child. It's stronger than the greatest greatness. It is more powerful than power. I was unaware of this ineffable phenomenon at the onset, and being unaware of it is its greatest weapon.

Not understanding this, many groups brought me in to speak to audiences about my incident and the practices we were sure helped. I traveled the country and spoke to as many people as possible about mental health.

I even went so far as to be on the front lines of the fight as a crisis counselor. Every time promoting the ways of the masses that we were convinced would work, but they never cracked the ineffable code.

This unexplainable phenomenon of wanting to kill myself was the foundation of thought when dealing with suicide during this time. After the white wisps, the bulbs bursting, and the blackening fade, I woke up into a human experience of both repetitive temporary healing and the evangelism of repetitive temporary healing. We were all bound together in futility. We told the world we brought hope, but we could not define the direction from which hope would be needed. We were lost, leading the lost. Charlatans of hope.

One major shift that happened for me was a set of two back-to-back crisis calls in a short time. The first was a young man who had just left the Marine Corps. He contacted me while struggling with thoughts of suicide after finding out two of his friends died in combat shortly after he left.

He started our talk in bad shape. His mind was overcome with survivor's guilt. Months went by while his emotional state steadily improved. One morning he talked with me about one of my projects he wanted to help with: nothing fancy, just a normal conversation.

He mentioned that if he could get funds together, he'd like to fly out and help with some of the things we were doing. I was willing to let people help. So, we had a decent and upbeat conversation, and then I told him I'd get back to him over the weekend to update him. It seemed simple enough. It was never simple enough.

I received a call later that evening - this young man, who had been in a good mood all day. Same as I was in my moment; he was not depressed then. He was sitting in his living room when his girlfriend in the kitchen heard a deafening pop. She ran into the room to see exactly what you think she saw.

She told me while crying through the phone that he somehow hung on for a few moments, but the clouds entered his eyes. He was fine for a moment, and then he was gone. He was fine that morning; he was fine for good. At least, that's what I told myself.

The next part of that jarring two-part shift came immediately after that young man committed suicide. I was contacted by a local police officer about a missing veteran who was rumored to be in my hometown.

He grabbed his backpack and left his house but didn't return. He was from a few states away, but the report was that he hitched a ride for a few hundred miles to come to my town. His fiancé and his parents were franticly searching for answers from anyone and anything.

After he went missing, an alert was put out for him, asking people to report if they knew anything of his whereabouts. They were alerted when his name was anonymously reported as checked into a group facility near me, hundreds of miles away from his home.

This alert put his family into a frenzy, which brought in the need for an investigator. The investigator contacted my local police department. However, this person had committed no crime. They couldn't just break into a group facility without knowing if the person they were looking for was inside.

I am still trying to understand what the law was and why the police could not go into the facility. From what I gathered; they needed a positive identification of him. Nevertheless, they asked me to get in and see if he was inside. Then they would be able to act.

That's what I did. For roughly six weeks, starting in the dead of winter, I became a wandering person without a home. That was the only way to get into many facilities. I became very familiar with that character; well played. Like the first act on a stage. Just looking for a man. He's lost, but we'll find him any day.

That character allowed me to meet many people who were struggling deeply. I'd never wish their life on anyone. I could not wait to get out of character and exit that stage.

Being that character had its comfort because I knew I could go back to my warm home at the end of the search. Though many of the people I met wanted to be there, many did not. Most had no hope. I never want to play that character again.

I had some friends help me go through tent cities and different facilities to help look for him. Every day I would talk to someone who said they knew where he was. So, I would go where they told me to go, but he would not be there.

I was in the tent cities, and I was under bridges. I was in group homes, I was stepping in human waste, and I saw all sorts of unimaginable things. I talked to people who wanted to be on the streets, while others never imagined they'd end up living like that. I saw everything, and I was everywhere I thought this man might be.

People from all over were giving me tips and information about where they last saw him. Hundreds of tips. There was so much hope that he would turn up that his family flew down to look for themselves.

Almost two months into this process, I got a call from the investigator in his hometown. He said, "Hey, I want to let you know we have found a body. It's near a train track close to his house, but it's not confirmed yet." It would be confirmed within an hour of that phone call.

I lost it. I have never felt so much anger. Every person and facility staff member who lied to his family and I had me fuming beyond any emotion I had ever felt. The false hope. I was done with crisis calls. I was done with people.

I was so angry with the world that I drove those hundreds of miles to his hometown to this man's funeral. I spent time with his mom and dad. I spent time with his fiancé and young son. I poured into every moment because they deserved that from all those people who gave them false hope. Everyone who lied and brought false hope should have been there to apologize. But they weren't. They didn't show up. They didn't care. They probably don't even know any of this happened!

The hardest part was that no matter how angry I got, it didn't bring him back. It didn't comfort his mother or father. His fiancé was still alone. His son was still without him.

I had to hear his mom crying his name and know that nothing I did or could have done could take that pain away from her. I wasn't even close. I had no power over this, and it crushed me. I was done with methods. I wanted the cure.

I had been looking for this man for a long time. I did not care that I sat in a funeral home and saw him there. I may have never met this man, but I did not recognize that as the man I was looking for. I decided at that moment I was going to find him wherever that journey took me. I was going to find me. The real me.

Before these two events, I had taken hundreds of crisis calls, possibly over a thousand had we counted. I heard everybody's worst day, every day. Seeing people at their worst moments in life and some of the worst situations. I saw it.

NO SAVING THE ALREADY DEAD

I was lying to myself each time, knowing that the ineffable was stronger than me. Each time I picked up the phone or met with someone struggling, I knew I had no chance when it arrived to take its keep.

There was no word, no allegiance, and no amount of donation money capable of wrestling death from the mind of the already dead. I saw this repeatedly. Full pockets, full caskets, full volume pleas from wounded mothers begging for truth to be fiction.

For every few successful crisis calls, I had "the one." Sometimes at that moment, they would be fine. Then, later, I would be called by their family, telling me they were gone. Wounded mothers. Wounded fathers. A war for wounded minds, but not a single warrior capable of winning the fight. Ineffable.

I know no words could save them because I spoke all the words. I know no allegiance saved them because they died still in allegiance. I know no human connection saved them because I watched them leave their families. I know this because of a catalog of studies over the years and hundreds of people. I wouldn't wish that catalog on anyone for any reason.

When it was my turn, the wisps, the bursting bulbs, and the blackening fog was a dim light that loomed in the distance. That powerful embrace of that woman holding me up, stopping my drop. There was a small boy through all the pressure and the drowning on dry land. My son.

He watched it all happen while standing in the garage doorway into our house. But, never once in that moment did his presence reconnect the fiber or cause me to stop what I was doing. That power, without definition, wrapped its roots around my mind.

I saw only light, shadow, and presence. No call from a friend, pill, allegiance, or emotion was strong enough to pull me from the electricity. Not even for you, son. I'm sorry. Ineffable.

In this box of evidence, I have numerous cases where the person was fine up until their final moment: the drop. I, too, followed this pattern. I saw stories upon stories of people saying, "we didn't see it coming!" Or "she was smiling and dancing only minutes prior!"

The answer to my dilemma was a momentum shift. When I was depressed and low, I lacked the motivation, desire, or motor functions to complete the act of killing myself. While I was depressed but upbeat, I had my motivation, desire, motor functions, and depression together in the same room. Explosive.

The low state of depression was acting as my guardian. The internal particles in my brain were bouncing around; my emotions followed suit. The mechanics of this drive were quite powerful and unrelenting.

It's not the greatest situation wholeness or peace would have been better. Also, not every case of suicide followed this pattern, as most were in deep depression and very low when they committed the act. But given the choice of life or death, my mind chose depression to slow me down long enough to possibly give it time to fix things. I didn't fix them in time.

Those handfuls of cases where that anomaly presented itself in tragic form bothered me, mainly because I had one of these anomalies as part of my story. Yet, every psychiatrist, psychologist, counselor, pastor, and whoever else I talked to would say no evidence supported my thesis. So, we all just went back to drugging people and doing awareness push-ups: the ways of the masses. That should fix it.

It's not working! It was never going to work! The path that I was on with crisis calls and doing stunts for awareness of suicide wasn't working; charlatans headed the whole act. All we came up with was, "call your friend," and do a stunt for social media and your virtue.

I witnessed many times when a friend would call a friend, both friends would come out the other side with seeds of depression that neither could define. Remember that doctor who told me that the stuff needed to go somewhere? He was talking to someone who could do something with what was being said to him. When we would call our friends, if they did not have the proper processing channels, we would only lump more negativity on them.

We even encouraged getting together to have some drinks with friends to cheer each other up. The madness to think that we could define the ineffable while drinking when we couldn't even define it sober.

Three weeks after that first young man took his life, his best friend, who had been a source of console, and a pallbearer at his funeral, took his life as well. We lost two when we should have never lost one. That scenario played out repeatedly. Yet, we vehemently said you needed to call a friend and vent. We paraded that strategy around in a championship parade. If we allowed one person to fall through the cracks by not reaching out in time, we heaped piles of regret onto ourselves for failing our friends. We turned madness into an art form.

Meanwhile, we talked about suicide so much that we turned it into a self-fulfilling prophecy for many. And we turned it into an answer for others. We created a monster. I watched as people who weren't even suicidal initially ended up dying at their own hands within a year. We created an environment where if you had a bad day, the answer to the equation of your sadness was "depression" and "suicide."

So, why am I talking about suicide again? Because it isn't fixed yet, at least not by the world. Almost nobody survives what I put my body through, and of those that do, hardly any have their faculties still in check. I had a million reasons to justify it and zero to stop me. Yet, I would later discover that I would have regretted dying.

Nothing would have stopped me; my wife barely found me in time, but nobody found that man from hundreds of miles away in time. Nobody found that young man or his best friend in time. The ways of the masses didn't fix it then. But now it is fixed in me and can be fixed in you.

CHAPTER 4

You Only Saw the Drop

I knew that if I was going to find the cure, I would ultimately have to define the ineffable. But how can I do that? The whole point of something being ineffable is that it cannot be defined. This mission is impossible. But I am impossible too. Something has to give. What was on my mind when I did it? When my wife walked out into the garage and saw me, she saw what the drop was. But that drop didn't really happen that day.

Everyone was surprised. How did you all not see this? Maybe I was too good at hiding it, or perhaps you only saw the drop. But I wasn't in the drop. That event started in a stairway of occurrences early in life. Each moment along the way was one step down, unseen on the scale of a lifetime but weighed full on the drop.

Some kids tricked me,
"Go into a tree house."
Pushed me out and then laughed. One Step.
In 5th grade, on Valentine's Day,
Gave cards to your valentine.
I got a card, it was blank, and they laughed. One step.
My first kiss, my sister's best friend.
I kissed her, but she barely made it through.
She had to do this "truth or dare." One step.

The kid was standing over me.
Punched down repeatedly.
Broken teeth and blood covered my face. One step.
Even still, I have dreams of going far.
But those towers fell,
Put my dreams on hold. One step.
A Marine, Now I am the fighter,
But one friend went down.
Why was he even there? One step.

Then another friend,
Then many more. My best friend,
More lost to war So many steps.
The ineffable took a few.
And even more found its power.
I sank deeper by the hour. One step.
I rebuilt it for a day.
With that diamond, my team.
But then they killed that dream.
One last step and all the small ones in between!

You looked for me in the drop.
But I wasn't in the drop.
I was in every step along the way,
Until the last step I ever wanted to take.

They will never listen because of one last call.
They will never listen because of loyalty at all.
They will never listen by begging them to stop.
The steps were already taken,
You only saw the drop.

EVERY STEP ALONG THE WAY

I didn't get to grieve appropriately because who knows how to mourn numerous violent deaths at that age, or ever? All I felt was guilt for feeling guilty, and I didn't even think I deserved the guilt in the first place. I have another step, and then another step, and then another step.

Are you currently in the last step you ever wanted to take? Or are you somewhere in the middle, making your way down here? Maybe you're higher? Look at the work you have.

Imagine if, along the way, those kids didn't do that to me. That's one step I have to take back. Imagine if you take your steps back. Imagine if you stop giving steps to others and they to you?

You are currently in the steps of others. You may have done some bad stuff to other people. I know I have. That's the whole point of what I am saying. If you're playing the victim in this suicide topic, you're ignoring that you have victimized others. It's impossible not to be in the steps of others.

I had to realize that I would be stuck in my cycle if I didn't start treating people better. You will be in that same cycle until you know you need to treat people better. Nobody is immune to this rule.

So, this whole thing is about moving forward in positivity? Yes, in a way. But a better way to say it is that you are in this moment in completeness and wholeness. You can't relive or pre-live your situations. You have to accept them for what they are, but it doesn't mean you can't change your present. It also doesn't mean you can't fix the mental processing of those situations.

The biggest takeaway is that if you ultimately end your life, you give one step to anybody affected by your death and then one more step each time they think they could have stopped you. The steps compound into gains upon gains of regret for them.

You solve nothing in your suicide. Your suicide becomes a genocide. One grave grows larger with each cut from the shovel. You hand out steps like fresh golden dandelions from the blowing seeds of the dead. Caught by the wind. Sowed into the ground by time: a cycle. The ineffable grows.

Suicide is a contagious virus, and it takes on whatever form it needs for each person it consumes. I am showing this in the story of the young man who had just left the Marine Corps and then took his life, followed by his friend taking his life as well.

Man has difficulty understanding it because the definition is fluid and relative to each. So, if you can't define your "self," you can't define suicide. No exceptions.

No matter how many friends you call, awareness stunts you post on social media, or heart-felt public emotional pleas you make. Without the definition, one step is handed to each one who hears you. Talking about it is worth a step in and of itself, which is curious for me to say as I am talking about it. But we can be done with it now.

So, what is the answer? Some say I shouldn't talk about this phenomenon of suicide. Like it hasn't been around for almost as long as humans. Some say I should talk about it more. Neither: you should discover who and what you are before you blow the seeds of a dandelion. Because when you answer the questions "who and what am I?" you solve most of the issues involved in suicide.

I solved the riddle, and no matter how adamant you may be that I not talk about it, what would that make me if I didn't tell anyone I could? I didn't want to write this, but then I realized that not explaining this would be pure evil and selfishness.

CHAPTER 5

Awakening Into the Calm

I decided that I needed something more than the same old stuff that everyone else was saying. I needed to find the cure, not just a muzzle. I needed to find a way out of my cycle. One morning I was lying on the floor with soft music playing in the background. I lay there calmly, trying to think of anything that could help. The longer I lay there, the more relaxed I became. I started to calm down to the point that I drifted into what I thought was a very real daydream. I was inside my mind, watching myself. It was so bizarre. What is this?

What I didn't realize was that I was so calm, so focused, that without even knowing what I was doing, I had slipped into a deep meditation. The calm was the most beautiful experience. I was in awe. I could see my thoughts coming and going. I pulled some old memories to see if it was possible. I saw things I hadn't thought about in years. It was amazing.

After some time, I came out of the moment and immediately looked up what had just happened. I was surprised that it was meditation and mindfulness. I had slipped into what is called metacognition. Or the awareness of my awareness. I was blown away. The more I researched, the more I realized that I should have been meditating for a long time. Maybe I had been.

My initial thought was that it couldn't be this simple. There has to be a pill or something, right? Eventually, you will find that this is the very first tiny step. There is so much to do beyond this moment. But you must take this first step to get to the cure: to become whole and find freedom.

Then, I discovered what neuroplasticity was. Neuroplasticity is the process by which your brain grows when you exercise it properly. You can use it negatively or positively. You will develop the fear-processing parts of your mind if you drive into fear without properly understanding how to handle emotions. Conversely, you will develop peace in your mind if you drive into peace by properly understanding how to become whole with your emotions. You choose.

I wanted to take on a more significant aspect of meditation. At first, I needed to figure out where to start. I downloaded a few guided meditation apps and tried them out, but I couldn't focus, and my mind kept wandering. I felt frustrated with myself. I felt like I was failing at something simple. But I didn't give up.

I decided to do more research and read up on meditation and the available techniques. I discovered that there are different types of meditation, like mindfulness meditation, loving-kindness meditation, and movement meditation. I also learned that it's normal for the mind to wander and that it's essential to forgive yourself when that happens.

With this brand-new understanding, I was able to approach meditation with a more open mind. I started with shorter sessions, just a few minutes at a time, and gradually built up into longer and deeper sessions.

It took time and patience, but I finally started to feel the benefits of meditation. I was able to be more present in the moment, more aware of my thoughts and emotions, and more able to let go of the things that were causing me stress. I also noticed that I slept better and was more energized during the day. You would love to be more relaxed and get better sleep, wouldn't you?

THE ANCIENT IS PRESENT

Meditation is an ancient practice that has been used for thousands of years to improve physical and mental health. Despite this, there is much aversion, mainly because people believe it is a religious practice.

Meditation is used by many prominent religions, which causes this confusion because the practice is not owned by religion. Still, it is a tool more closely related to stretching or a gym workout than religion.

Some benefits of meditation include reducing stress and anxiety, improving focus and concentration, and promoting overall well-being. Also, like working out in a gym, your brain becomes more robust through neuroplasticity. Meditation can also be used in other contexts, such as studying for a high school exam or learning new skills and trades.

I had been meditating almost my entire life and didn't know. I learned various skill sets by setting them in front of me and meditating on them for hours a day, weeks on end, for months into years. There are different types of meditation, each with its unique focus and benefits. But with that, I focused on only a few.

Mindfulness Meditation

Mindfulness meditation involves focusing on the present moment and being aware of your thoughts, feelings, and sensations. It can be done in any position, whether sitting, standing, or walking. By focusing on the present moment and being non-judgmental about the thoughts that come and go, you can let go of stress and anxiety.

Mindfulness meditation is a practice that can help you become more aware of your thoughts and emotions and learn to observe them without judgment. If your mind begins to wander, gently bring your attention back to your breath. You may notice that your thoughts come and go like clouds in the sky. Simply observe them without getting caught up in them.

You may notice patterns in your thoughts and emotions as you continue practicing. You may also start seeing how specific thoughts and emotions affect your body and overall well-being.

By observing your thoughts and emotions this way, you can gain more control over them and make conscious choices about how you want to respond. You will find that you are less reactive and more present in each moment. With practice, you can strengthen this powerful tool and begin to live a more balanced and fulfilled life.

Contemplative Meditation

Contemplative meditation is a powerful tool for self-reflection and understanding. It involves taking time to reflect on a specific topic or idea and can be used as a form of reflective thinking that allows you to gain insight into yourself, others, and any perspective in any direction of your focus.

People from various faiths use this type of meditation as a form of prayer. Regardless of your background, with contemplative meditation, you focus on a specific person or situation to gain greater compassion and understanding.

One of the key benefits of contemplative meditation is that it allows you to slow down and take a step back from the constant chatter of your mind. It provides an opportunity to focus on something more meaningful and to be present in the moment. This can be particularly beneficial for gaining perspective on your thoughts and emotions, allowing you to observe them without judgment or attachment.

Additionally, contemplative meditation can be used as a tool for gaining focus on a particular topic. Whether it's an issue related to personal growth, a problem at work, or a relationship, taking time to reflect on the subject in a contemplative state can lead to greater insight and understanding.

Contemplative meditation is effective for gaining self-awareness, compassion, and perspective in any direction of your focus. It is a valuable tool for personal growth and understanding and can be used in various aspects of life.

This meditation is similar to transcendental meditation, which I will touch on next. The key difference is that whereas transcendental meditation is a mantra-based meditation practice focusing on one small item in repetition, contemplative meditation is based more on the whole concept of which you want to gain a greater understanding. You have a more free-flowing presence inside and around the whole concept, not just one single section or part of it in repetition. You can see a powerful strategy with these practices when set into a sequence.

First, you use contemplative meditation to focus on the overall subject and gain a broad understanding of the material. You sit comfortably and focus on your breath, allowing your mind to clear and become more open to the information. Then, you review the material in your mind, trying to understand the main concepts and how they relate.

Once you have a broad understanding of the whole section, transition to transcendental meditation to gain a more detailed understanding of one specific topic or concept, this allows your mind to drive deep into understanding.

Transcendental Meditation

Transcendental meditation is a technique that involves sitting comfortably with your eyes closed and focusing on a chosen mantra, repeating it mentally. The goal is to reach a state of pure consciousness or "transcendental awareness" and reduce stress and anxiety.

Usually, this type of meditation is learned through a series of personal instruction sessions with a guide. It is a simple technique, no matter your age or background.

A practical way to approach this type of meditation is to pick something simple and quick that you can easily repeat in your mind. Sit comfortably with your eyes closed and focus on the chosen mantra. The goal is to repeat the mantra mentally, allowing your mind to settle into a deeper state of relaxation and reducing stress and anxiety.

Repeating the mantra will help to quiet the mind, allowing you to transcend or go beyond your thinking mind and reach a state of pure consciousness or "transcendental awareness." This can be a powerful tool for self-discovery and understanding yourself or any perspective in any direction of your focus. You should approach this type of meditation in your own meaningful way.

Loving-Kindness Meditation

Loving-kindness meditation focuses on developing feelings of love and compassion for yourself and others by silently repeating phrases that promote love and compassion towards yourself and others. I use this method more as a prayer of compassion and mercy for myself or someone than anything else.

Similar to contemplative and transcendental meditation, this can be used in prayer. However, contemplative meditation is a broader view and focuses on a topic, issue, or situation; transcendental meditation is driving deeper, while loving-kindness meditation is about the person without any ties to a narrative.

This is a practical type of meditation that can be done at any time in almost any situation. You can even think of it as a daydream about someone in a positive manner. This is the type of meditation that is referred to when people say, "sending positive vibes your way."

You can use this to end a session where you started with contemplative meditation and then moved into transcendent meditation. It's a great way to seal the moment with compassion. Try using all three sometime, either in prayer or if you're not from a faith perspective, use them toward someone you love.

Guided Imagery Meditation

Guided imagery meditation is a form of meditation in which you are guided through a visualization process, typically by a recorded voice or a live guide. I have a section in this message where I walk you through some guided imagery to build the framework for your eventual victory. So, be ready for that guided imagery exercise when you get to it.

The visualization often involves creating a mental image of a peaceful scene or scenario, such as a serene beach or a quiet forest.

Guided imagery meditation aims to help you relax, reduce stress and anxiety, and promote overall well-being.

During a guided imagery meditation session, you are usually instructed to close your eyes and focus on your breath. The guide then leads you through a series of descriptive prompts, calmly encouraging you to imagine different aspects of the scene.

Guided imagery meditation can be helpful for various issues, like stress, anxiety, pain management, and insomnia. The mental images can help you defeat negative thoughts and emotions, promote relaxation, and ease the tension anxiety causes on your body and mind.

Moving Meditation

I spoke to a good friend right before completing this writing. I talked to him about the benefits of meditation. My friend was a Green Beret and had extensive knowledge about mental exercises and performance under intense pressure.

I used this opportunity to pick his mind about heightened awareness practices during high-intensity events in his former career as a Green Beret and now in his current career as a reality competition show host. When I asked him if he practiced meditation, he replied, "It's not for me. That's what I have the gym for". It makes sense, I get it, and I respect that.

I came from this same mindset. In my former life with athletics, then in the Marine Corps, I understood the principles used in the gym. I also know that one of the most important principles is breathing. Spend one minute with a personal trainer while lifting weights in a gym, and you are guaranteed to be reminded to breathe. If you hold your breath while lifting, they reflexively shout, "breathe!"

My friend gets his therapy by focusing on the physical gym while breathing and moving physically measured heavy things. In contrast, I get my therapy in my mental gym while breathing and moving mentally measured heavy things.

As I was talking to my friend, I couldn't help but notice we were saying the same thing from two separate rooms in the same house. What if there was a way to combine both? What if they are already connected?

I needed a way to reach my friend and others with this message of hope without bludgeoning people's ideals but instead meeting them in their moment to uncover these forgotten and hidden principles. It occurred to me that I may not have to say anything at all. Don't fix what isn't broken.

I learned that principle as a baseball coach. When I would have a player hitting for a high average but with a goofy swing, I wouldn't say anything to him, "don't fix what isn't broken." The same thing applies to my friend in our conversation about weightlifting and meditation practices.

There is no need for me to beat him down with meditation if he is already doing it. The very mention of the concept of "meditation in weightlifting" is enough to plant a seed to grow and bear fruit in its time.

My friend is already unknowingly using his own variation of dynamic or moving meditation. He focuses on his muscles, centering on the process while breathing and remaining locked into himself and his goal.

Now with a greater understanding of what the mind is doing during weightlifting, if you're a weightlifter or perform any type of physical exercise. You, too, can tap into the unlimited power of your mind. Using the resources that have always been within reach of your hands: physical and mental.

Moving meditation is a form of meditation that involves incorporating movement and physical activity into practice. The idea behind moving meditation is to use the body's movement to focus the mind and bring attention to the present moment. By focusing on the activity and sensation of the body, you can let go of distracting thoughts and emotions and find a sense of inner peace and tranquility.

To practice moving meditation, begin by focusing on your breath and body as you move. You can start by doing simple stretches or walking around your neighborhood, focusing on the sensation of your feet hitting the ground and the air on your skin. As you move, try to let go of any distracting thoughts or worries and focus solely on the sensation of your body. You can also incorporate mindful breathing techniques to help you stay present and focused.

Moving meditation has many benefits, including reducing stress and anxiety.

NAVIGATING THE JOURNEY

It's important to note that the practice of meditation can be different for each individual, and there is no one-size-fits-all approach. It's also important to remember that meditation is a practice, and it takes time to develop the skill of meditation and start reaping its benefits. So, don't get discouraged if you have difficulty focusing or if your mind wanders at first.

Regular meditation practice can lead to a decrease in symptoms of anxiety and depression and an improvement in overall well-being. Regular meditation practice can decrease your symptoms of anxiety and depression as well as lower your blood pressure and improve immune function.

So, how do you get started with meditation? The best way to start is to find a quiet and comfortable place where you won't be disturbed. Then, set a timer for a few minutes and focus on your breath. You can also try guided meditations found online or through meditation apps. I'll give you a simple starting point for meditation.

Find a quiet and comfortable space where you can sit or lie down undisturbed. Sit or lie down comfortably, keeping your back straight, and your body relaxed. Close your eyes.

Take a few deep breaths. Focus on the sensation of the air entering and leaving your body. Breathe in while counting slowly to four. Let it out while counting slowly to six. Bring your attention to your breath. Do this until you start to calm down. Focus on the sensation of your breath as it enters and leaves your nose or mouth.

If your mind starts to wander, gently bring your attention back to your breath. Don't judge yourself for getting lost in your thoughts, and it's natural to do so. If your thoughts wander, recognize them and come back to your breath.

Allow your breath to return to its natural pattern. Notice how it changes, and your diaphragm isn't inflating as much. Feel the breath coming in and going out of you. Do this for as long as you like.

Remain calm and quiet and practice breathing and refocusing from distractions. When you're done, slowly open your eyes and take a moment in your position. After you finish, take a moment to notice how you feel before getting up.

You can use this for a while until you better manage your thoughts. Start with a short meditation, 5-10 minutes, and gradually increase the time as you get comfortable with the practice. Your mind, through neuroplasticity, will become strong in time, and those thoughts will have a more challenging time breaking into your moment.

Meditation can be a powerful tool for improving physical and mental health. Whether you're looking to reduce stress and anxiety, improve focus and concentration, or achieve a greater sense of inner peace, there's a type of meditation that can help. Remember to be patient with yourself as you learn this skill and regularly practice for the best results.

Something strange happened to me when meditation became an everyday occurrence. I realized that in that garage that night. The breakers in my mind were being flipped. I was waiting for the final one to shut me off. My wife stopped that final breaker, but every step back from that moment reset all those breakers.

Interestingly, I have found entire sets of breakers that were never being used prior. My circuits were healing; the circuit board was growing with more circuits and even entire breaker boards. I was increasing the scale of my mind through meditation.

As much as I first loved meditation, I knew there was more. I knew that despite experiencing healing, there was more to do. Meditation is not the total answer but the start of the journey. It's an essential yet simple step that you can do for a few minutes while lying in bed in the morning or before bed at night.

WHAT IS PRESENT IS PEACE

Mindfulness is a state of active, open attention to the present. It involves paying attention to what is happening in the present moment without judgment. It's a way of engaging in the current experience with curiosity, openness, and without judgment or distraction. It's a skill you can develop through practice, allowing you to experience the present moment in a non-reactive way.

Mindfulness can help you to be more aware of your thoughts, emotions, and physical sensations and to respond to them in a more balanced and effective way. It can help to reduce stress and anxiety, improve concentration, and increase emotional regulation.

This practice can be used in almost any situation, whether during daily activities, in nature, or a formal setting like a yoga or meditation class. The important thing is to pay attention to the present moment with an open and non-judgmental attitude.

A friend of mine recently told me that he was struggling with PTSD, but he noticed that holding his newborn son felt like it healed his mind. "It does!" I exclaimed. I was so happy to hear him say this because he was unlocking the benefit of mindfulness while he centered his focus entirely on his son. That moment was healing for him. He should do it more and never stop.

I've had some incredibly profound moments during mindfulness. One of my first "wow" moments was when I felt like time had collapsed. I began to have this overwhelming sense that this existence was not a tick on a linear timeline, but instead: I am here. I thought I was in eternity, and my awareness of being alive collapsed the constant eternal wave into my present existence.

This moment moved from deep mindfulness to deep meditation, where I became so fixed on this function of time that I found myself inside a new world. I found all the fibers and connectors of my mind, but they were not what I expected. I could see them working and moving.

I could watch my mind work, but I wasn't sure if my mind knew I was there, so I asked for a random memory. I wanted it to be one I hadn't thought of in many years. Instantly, I had in front of me a screen and a memory from fifth grade. Something I had not even thought of for many years. I was in awe.

This moment altered my life so profoundly that nothing remained the same, nor has anything returned to the same before that moment. I was experiencing healing. I was discovering my "self." I was at the door. I entered.

THE POWER OF PRESENCE

Mindfulness and meditation are two of the most valuable tools you can use on your journey of self-discovery. They help you become more self-aware and understand who you are, your thoughts, emotions, and physical sensations.

When practicing mindfulness and meditation, you may find it challenging to focus and quiet your mind, but don't be discouraged. With consistent practice, you will see gradual improvements. As you focus on the present moment and observe your thoughts and emotions without judgment, you will become more understanding of yourself and others.

One of the most transformative aspects of mindfulness and meditation is their ability to help you work through negative emotions like anger, fear, and guilt. By learning to be present and non-judgmental with yourself, you will find it easier to let go of these emotions and find peace. This increased self-awareness helps you understand your needs and wants better.

Mindfulness and meditation can also improve your relationships with others. By becoming more present and understanding in your interactions with others, you will be able to communicate more effectively and build stronger connections.

Incorporating mindfulness and meditation into your daily routine can have a positive impact on other areas of your life as well. It helps you be more productive at work and enhances your ability to enjoy simple pleasures. Take the time to find a practice that works for you and embrace the journey.

The benefits of mindfulness and meditation are endless and can be genuinely transformative. From increased self-awareness to improved relationships, they offer the opportunity to understand yourself and others better. So, take the time to be present and see what unfolds for you as you delve deeper into mindfulness and meditation. You may discover the audacity to win, just like I did. The possibilities are endless, and you may be surprised at what you find.

With these benefits in mind, it's time to challenge yourself to take the initiative for self-discovery. The path to self-discovery is not always easy, but it is worth it. By embracing mindfulness and meditation, you can start to uncover the answers to questions about yourself that you may have never considered before. This journey of self-discovery requires courage, but the rewards are limitless. So, take the first step; this is your opportunity to uncover your unique path. I found the brazen audacity to win. Will you?

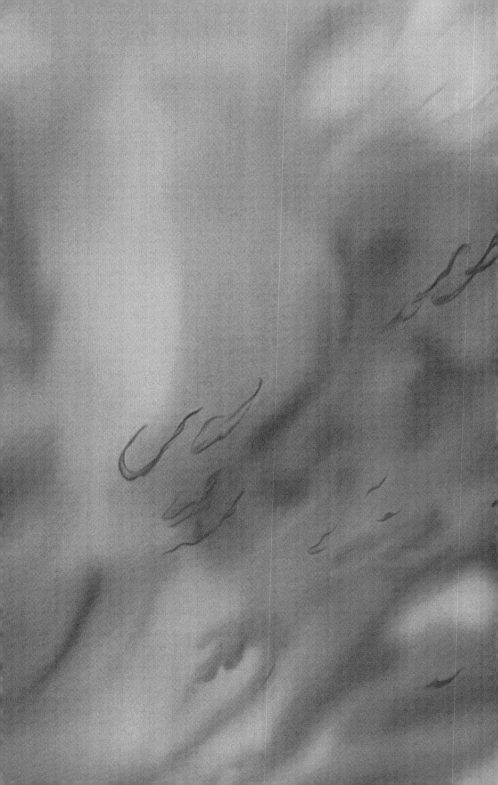

CHAPTER 6

It's Your Turn

Even with this deep meditation and mindfulness, I felt like there was more to the story. I felt this way mainly because I was gaining a grasp on my sense of self but struggling with communication with others. So, I started digging deeper into both practices, and it became apparent that I needed to understand emotions and perceptions even more.

If you want to walk through that door, you must understand how your emotions work. They are integral to healing your mind and taking control of your life, emotions, and ultimately you.

Creating a map of your emotions and seeing what they are and what they do for you allows you to follow the information trail in your mind. Though I do not intend to explore every aspect of your mind and emotions in this message, I am here to create a starting point for you.

USE EMOTIONS TO YOUR ADVANTAGE

Your emotions also have a physical component. When you feel happy, you might notice your heart rate increase and your facial muscles relax. When you feel angry or sad, you might notice your muscles tense up and your heart rate increase.

Emotions also play a role in your memory. When you experience a powerful emotion, your brain is more likely to remember the event and its details. This is why you might remember a particularly happy event or maybe a traumatic experience from your past more vividly than a neutral one.

Emotions are a complex and integral part of who you are. They help you understand and navigate any direction of your focus around you and play a role in shaping your memories and experiences.

Like the step-by-step process I addressed earlier when I showed you how multiple events brought me to the drop, emotions can often work similarly. They start as an insignificant feeling that you don't deal with properly, and then another one enters and compounds on top of the first.

In time, those emotions build on top of each other to form a powerful product of change in your life. If they are negative, the change agent will be damaging. So, it is crucial to understand and know them intimately so you can manage them properly.

Happiness

I'll start with happiness. Happiness is a good feeling you get when things are going well. It can be great because it makes you feel good and can make you healthier. But too much happiness can also be harmful because it can make you lazy.

This emotion is also where I differ from many who teach about the principles of the mind. I do not believe a constant state of happiness is healthy. Wholeness and completeness are healthy; peace is healthy. Happiness is an emotion, and if it overtakes your life, you do not have control over it; it has power over you. That is not proper, no matter how nice happiness can feel. So, treat it kindly, but make sure to manage it properly.

It's essential to try and understand where your happiness comes from and to appreciate the good things in your life. And remember, happiness comes and goes; it isn't always going to be there.

One way to make yourself happier is to start writing in a gratitude journal. Write down three things you're grateful for in the morning. You could also use a notetaking app. Most phones come with a notetaking app. This can help you focus on the good stuff and make you happier. When was the last time you were happy? What was the reason? How long did the happiness last?

Sadness

Sadness is an emotion of disappointment and loss triggered by events like bad news, loss, or feelings of loneliness. Although sadness can have both positive and negative impacts, it's important to manage it effectively to avoid depression.

Positive aspects of sadness include processing difficult experiences, building empathy, and fostering self-discovery and growth. However, overwhelming sadness can lead to depression, lack of motivation, and strain on relationships and daily life.

Remember the doctor initially told me that physical activity would help with sadness and depression? It did help. It wasn't the whole story, though. I had to dig deeper than just fixing emotions. As with all emotions, they have a root cause that must be managed. Regular physical activity can increase the release of endorphins, chemicals in the brain that help improve mood and reduce stress.

Sadness is a normal emotion that can positively and negatively affect your life. It can be a way to process difficult experiences and emotions, build empathy, and inspire growth and self-discovery. However, it can also lead to feelings of hopelessness and depression if left unmanaged.

Anger

Anger is a normal emotion you experience. But what if anger starts to control your life? Anger can have both positive and negative effects. When used correctly, it can motivate and help you set boundaries with others. However, if not managed well, it can lead to destructive behaviors, harm relationships, and even cause long-term health issues.

I recall a man in my group therapy session who shared when he realized the power of anger. He got angry with his wife and, before she could leave to cool down, he smashed a full milk jug on her head, causing major injury. This shocked me and made me even more aware of the dark side of anger.

It's important to learn how to control anger to avoid negative consequences. I have chosen to abstain from anger as much as possible.

People often say venting is a way to release anger, but it's a dangerous lie. Venting anger to others can lead to unnecessary conflicts, hurt feelings, and even worsen the situation. Anger is also a contagious emotion, and venting only fuels it. Instead, take time to cool down before talking to anyone, write down your thoughts, or practice physical exercise, meditation, or yoga to reduce anger. When was the last time you were angry?

Fear

"Misery loves company," and so does anger. It's a common partner with fear. Fear, just like anger, can have both positive and negative effects. On the one hand, fear is a natural emotion that keeps you safe and alert and can inspire you to achieve your goals. But, when fear takes over, it can lead to anxiety, stress, and phobias and even hold you back from living a peaceful life.

One way to manage your fear is by facing your fears and understanding coping mechanisms. Another way is by practicing mindfulness and meditation. It's essential to remember that fear is a normal emotion, and you will experience it often in your life and most likely already have.

Using fear as a motivator is a common tactic used by managers, but it's not always the best approach. Fear may work in the short term, but it can negatively affect people in the long run. It's your responsibility to understand the people around you and what motivates them, as fear may only work for some of them.

Think back to the last time you felt fear. Was it a good or bad experience? How did you react during and after that experience?

Positive Surprise

Fear has a cousin: surprise. Many of the same actions in your brain with fear happen with surprise. Surprise is that feeling you get when something unexpected happens. It's a neutral emotion that can evoke different reactions depending on the situation. But like any other emotion, surprise can also have positive and negative effects on your life.

Let's start with the positive effects of surprise. Surprise can be a source of excitement and adventure; it can also help to break the monotony and bring new and fresh perspectives. It can also be of help to open up new opportunities and experiences.

Surprise can also be a way to learn and grow, as it can help you to be more flexible and adaptable to change.

One of my first significant investments into a business I had started. I had been working with a worldwide manufacturer for months to transition one of their in-house departments into a spin-off company. I worked for months to ensure everything was in order and ready to move.

However, they canned the project, which made all my work useless. They didn't want anything to do with it anymore. They even signed over all intellectual property to me for my use however I wanted.

About a year later, I got an email from what I assumed was a scammer. He wanted to buy one of those items and was willing to pay a large sum. He stated that this was his last offer and then he would be moving on.

I was confused, but I checked my emails and found that this man had indeed been emailing me for months, trying to buy this particular piece of intellectual property, but

I had never seen any of the emails, and there were plenty of emails. I never entertain these approaches, but for some reason, this one felt different from any other.

In each email, he raised the amount he was willing to pay. He thought I was a tough negotiator by not responding, but I never saw any of those emails! With some legal paperwork, I vetted this person, and then we set up an escrow to ensure a fair transaction. I sent him the intellectual property. To my surprise, I woke up one morning with a large amount of money in my account.

To my even bigger surprise, five months later, I saw the intellectual property in a Super Bowl commercial from a major company. I could have asked for a lot more money. Nevertheless, it was one small surprise.

Negative Surprise

On the other hand, surprise can also negatively affect your life. When a surprise is unexpected and unpleasant, it can lead to feelings of shock or distress. If the surprise is terrible and severe, it can lead to long-term emotional and mental effects like anxiety or depression. Sometimes surprises can also be a source of stress, especially when unprepared for them. When life doesn't go as planned, you can plan on stress.

My boss and I were on the way to a meeting when the sheriff's officer stopped us to hand me the packet. I knew what it was, and my boss knew what it was. I didn't need to look inside. I was being served divorce papers. This was not a good surprise.

However, we had a big meeting we were walking to, and I didn't have time to worry about this packet. So, for that 5-minute walk, which included an elevator ride, I unfocused my eyes, set my mind internally, and focused on my breathing. Then I transitioned to a body scan while walking by noticing the sensation of my feet inside of my shoes hitting the pavement.

Anytime a thought tried to attack me, I acknowledged it, then moved it aside. I performed a few more simple tasks related to multiple types of meditation and mindfulness in that short walk to the boardroom, then BOOM! My mind jumped into something fantastic.

I was laser focused when we arrived in the conference room. I'm sure it appeared to others that I had zoned out. I had zoned out, but not into a daydream. I had placed myself in such a hyper-aware state that it is called "the zone." In this zone, all of my faculties were working. Nothing had a level higher than anything else.

Every voice in the room was on the same level as my heartbeat. Every scratch of a pen was equal with each breath. My mind was not blocking any of my abilities. I was, at this moment, more capable of greatness than at any other moment. Finding the ability to engage this zone with the snap of a finger became one of my main objectives from this point on.

Athletes use it, businesspeople use it, inventors use it, and authors use it. But this initial snap of the finger instance was spurred on by the negative side of surprise.

It's important to remember that surprise is a normal emotion and can be a source of growth and learning. By learning to manage your reactions to surprise, you can avoid negative consequences and use them to your advantage.

Disgust

Disgust is an emotional response triggered by negative things such as unpleasant odors, spoiled food, or unacceptable behavior. While it can be a natural protective mechanism, disgust can also have negative consequences such as hatred, phobias, and prejudice.

On the positive side, disgust can serve as a defense mechanism that helps protect against potential harm. It can also help maintain social norms by creating boundaries and promoting acceptable behavior.

However, when disgust becomes too much to handle, it can lead to negative consequences, such as limiting your ability to try new things, promoting discrimination and prejudice, and resulting in hate. Hate is born from disgust.

One way to manage disgust is to understand its source and learn more about it. Another way is to practice mindfulness and focus on the present moment. It's important to remember that disgust is a normal emotion.

By learning to manage your disgust, you can avoid negative consequences and use them to your advantage. And also, it is essential to remember that disgust can be a way to protect yourself.

Contempt

Contempt is disrespect triggered by destructive behavior or attitudes. While it can negatively affect you by promoting hate, it can also be used positively to drive change. It's like a courtroom where you can argue your case yet be held in contempt when you get out of line.

Contempt can be a way to hold people accountable for their actions. It can also be a way to maintain healthy relationships.

On the other hand, contempt can transition into anger and lead to conflicts. It can also lead to a negative self-perception and negative self-talk.

So, how do you manage your contempt? One way is to understand the source of your contempt and learn more about it. Another way is to practice compassion and see things from the other person's perspective. It's important to remember that contempt is a normal emotion, but it's essential to learn how to control it.

By learning to manage your contempt, you can avoid negative consequences and use them to your advantage. And also, it is essential to remember that contempt should not be used to harm others but rather to hold them accountable respectfully.

Shame

Shame is a negative emotion driven by inadequacy or self-consciousness that you get when you feel like you've failed. But like any other emotion, shame can also have positive and negative effects on your life.

Shame can be a way to hold yourself accountable for your actions. It can also be a way to learn from your mistakes and grow from them. Shame can also motivate and inspire you to make positive changes in your life.

Shame can also have adverse effects on your life. When shame becomes overwhelming, it can lead to feelings of worthlessness. It can also lead to self-deprecation and then to self-hate.

So, how do you manage your shame? One way is to understand the source of your shame and learn more about it. Another way is to practice self-compassion and be kind to yourself.

It's important to remember that shame is a normal emotion, but by learning to manage it, you can avoid negative consequences and use them to your advantage.

You should not use shame to harm yourself. Instead, hold yourself accountable respectfully and learn from your mistakes to avoid making them anymore.

Guilt

Guilt is an intense emotion of remorse or responsibility for something that has gone wrong or for a behavior that is not acceptable.

Guilt can motivate you to make positive changes in your behavior and make amends for your wrongdoings. It can also hold you accountable for your actions and help you learn from your mistakes.

However, when guilt overwhelms, it can have negative consequences, such as feelings of worthlessness and negative self-talk. Constant guilt can strain relationships and lead to conflicts. In severe cases, guilt can become a source of obsession, dominating your thoughts and emotions, such as survivor's guilt, which arises from the feeling of why you survived while others did not.

Managing guilt requires you to understand its source and to practice self-compassion. Guilt is normal, but learning to control it is essential to avoid negative consequences. By learning how to manage guilt, you can use it to your advantage and hold yourself accountable respectfully while learning from your mistakes.

Guilt is a powerful emotion that can positively and negatively affect your life. By learning to manage guilt, you can avoid negative consequences and use it to your advantage.

Envy

Many people view envy as a source of inspiration rather than a negative emotion. It is resentment towards someone else's possessions or abilities and is often triggered by seeing someone else's success, possessions, or abilities.

This emotion can quickly become damaging if left unchecked. Without warning, it can lead to feelings of inadequacy, low self-esteem, and strain in relationships.

While envy may appear to have some positive aspects, it is important to learn how to manage it to avoid negative consequences.

Understanding the source of your envy and practicing gratitude can help you control your envy. It is also important to remember that envy should not be used to harm others.

It is normal to experience envy, but learning how to control it is crucial. By learning to manage your envy, you can avoid negative consequences and even use it to your advantage.

It is important to remember that envy is just one of many emotions, and many others can impact our thoughts and behaviors. Attaching a name to these emotions and understanding their basic purpose and impact on our lives can help us navigate them more effectively.

POSITIVITY

Positivity is about focusing on the good in every situation, searching for silver linings, and finding opportunities in challenges, not ignoring the negative parts of life.

So, why is positivity important for your well-being? There's a theory that a positive mindset can lead to a more positive descriptive style.

Instead of attributing negative events to permanent, uncontrollable, and universal factors, you can see them as temporary, specific, and changeable elements. This thinking can help you be more resilient and cope better in adverse situations.

Moreover, positive emotions can broaden your perspective and help you see new possibilities and opportunities in your life and others. So, how can you cultivate positivity in your life? It's simple. Focus on the good in every situation, cultivate positive emotions, practice resilience, and continuously reflect on and adjust your mindset to be positive.

Remember, positivity has a powerful impact on your well-being. It can help you be more resilient, broaden your perspective, and see new opportunities. So, as you go through your day, keep positivity in mind and choose to incorporate it into your life. With positivity on your side, you can tackle any challenge that comes your way.

NEGATIVITY

Do you feel weighed down by negativity in your daily life? Your brain is wired to pay more attention to negative things, but you can change that. Let's examine negativity bias and learn practical strategies to shift your focus towards positivity and improve your overall well-being.

The world can often seem overwhelmingly negative, with more descriptors for negative interactions than positive ones. Dealing with negativity from people and events can be challenging. However, it's important to understand that your brain's negative bias is a survival mechanism that helped our ancestors avoid potential dangers. Negative information is processed more thoroughly and elicits a stronger emotional response than positive information, making it more likely to be remembered. This negative bias can also extend to social interactions, leading you to remember and dwell on negative experiences more than positive ones.

But don't worry; you can train your brain to focus on the positive. One way to do this is by keeping a gratitude journal and expressing gratitude to others. Practicing mindfulness, being present and fully engaged in the current moment, can also help you appreciate the small things in life and shift your focus towards positivity.

It's normal for your brain to pay more attention to negative things. Still, by implementing practical strategies such as gratitude journaling and mindfulness, you can train your brain to focus on the positive and improve your well-being. Everyone responds to negativity differently, but these strategies can provide a starting point for many people.

Take control of your thoughts and emotions by recognizing the power of negativity bias in your life. Don't let negativity dictate your emotions. By shifting your focus towards positivity and embracing gratitude and mindfulness, you can move towards a more positive and fulfilling life. Do you feel that you tend to be more negative than positive? Start making changes today and take control of your thoughts and emotions.

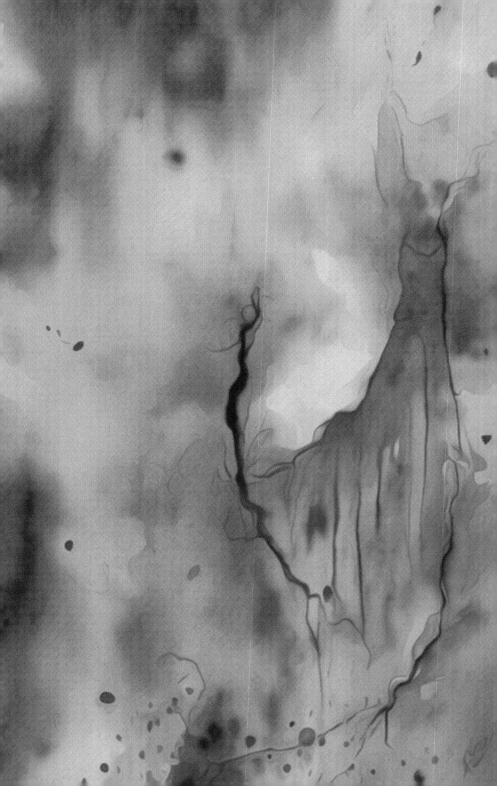

CHAPTER 7

Damage Control

You may think you're not suffering, but human existence guarantees suffering, even if small. I had to ask myself these questions as well. They are part of the process of self-discovery, in that finding out where you are suffering can be a trail that leads you directly to your suffering. Once you find your suffering, then you can deal with it.

The only way to cease suffering is to admit that you have suffered, even if it is small. Once you come to that truth, you will move to the cause of the suffering. You must decide if you believe the suffering can cease when you see the reason. If you think it can cease, and you understand that the path exists and is at your feet, you will be at the door. But the first part of that is admitting and describing your suffering.

QUESTION ONE

Are you someone who typically does the right thing? Sometimes, even when you help someone or do something good, you may be taken advantage of or receive negative reactions. The saying "no good deed goes unpunished" refers to this phenomenon.

I worked at a small yet successful company. It was my first salary-compensated position and my first official director title. I was so proud of myself for this achievement. I had a little office, ten by ten in a little square, and the door faced out to a commons area for another department which included a few desks.

Outside my door was a desk for a lady in that other department; I didn't communicate much with her, but we got along reasonably well. She goes away on medical leave. I only knew she went on medical leave because another coworker came up to me and said, "Hey, did you hear she went on medical leave because she tried to kill herself?" This was not something I should have been told, but I had to hear that, and there was nothing I could have done to prevent hearing it.

A bit later, another employee is annoyed that she has to do extra work. She states that it's because that lady is away on medical leave for attempting to kill herself. I can't do anything with this information. It does not affect me at all. The office gossip gave it to me. This happened many times while she was away, and the mood of those in her department grew increasingly negative about her absence.

That lady returned to work many days later, and everyone was happy to see her. They all told her how much they missed her and how much they had been thinking about her. Some even said they had been "praying" for her to other people in conversation. I suppose gossiping and complaining about her could be considered thinking about her?

I was annoyed by this, but they're a different department, so I didn't get too deep into the situation. However, that slight negativity does change my attitude slightly. I became a bit irritable with people during that workday. The negativity compounded with each conversation.

That lady was sitting in her chair, her back facing me right outside my office. Just then, my boss entered my office and shut my door with a big goofy smile. He looked at me with his big grin and thumb, pointing in her direction, and said, "she needs a wider chair."

I was already annoyed and didn't think it was appropriate for him to say that, so I told him that. I should have said nothing, but my negative attitude was hard to fight. Even more, I didn't know how to fight a negative mindset.

This wasn't the first time my boss had said this or something similar about people. I had been at this company for a year, and it had always been like this with him. My boss had been there for ten years. As far as I could tell by how people spoke about him at the office, it had always been a part of his routine.

I have always believed that if somebody's talking to you about other people, they are talking to others about you. Just like those people gossiped about that lady. Do you have someone like that in your life? Are you that person? This exchange made a bit of an awkward moment between my boss and me. It was the right thing to do then, but we quickly moved on.

I got called into the owner's office the next day. My boss is there too. The owner looks at us and says, "Hey, I've noticed that you two have a little bit of animosity toward each other lately. Things aren't clicking, and We're not running on all cylinders. What's going on between you two?"

Knowing what happened just the day prior, I brought that up as a small example of what it's like dealing with that man.

So, part of my anger towards him was for what he said about that lady, but it was also self-serving because I knew he was doing that about me too, but to other people. So, I wasn't exactly a white knight there. I had some skin in the game.

But I was also annoyed that all those people were gossiping about her. Then they acted as if they had only said nice things about her.

When the owner asked what the problem was, I brought up the incident from the day prior. I told him I didn't know if I'd buy into my boss's leadership style. I thought that would earn me some respect from the owner because I did the right thing.

He asked my boss about what I said, and to my surprise, he did not try to weasel out of his tasteless joke but instead denied he ever said it. So, I thought the owner and I would debate our following actions. Nope. He looked at me and said, "We can't have liars here. Aaron, get your stuff and get out." I was fired on the spot.

I did the right thing, which didn't go well because no good deed goes unpunished. My suffering, in that instance, came from the disruption of my attachment to my sense of virtue. I knew I did the right thing, but the calamity all rested in my mind. Have you ever done the right thing, and it didn't go well for you? What attachments to "self" were apparent, and what emotions came about because of your suffering?

QUESTION TWO

Have you been successful in life or your career but feel like you've plateaued? Is that something to which you can relate? You've worked hard to get where you are in life. You've climbed the corporate ladder, built a successful business, or achieved a level of success in your field. This could even include general life experiences like maybe you start to feel good, but then one of those negative emotions from earlier starts to creep in, and you find yourself sad or even emotionless.

You had a high point, but now, you feel like you've hit a plateau. You've risen, but now it's just a flat line in life. You can't figure out what's next or how to keep moving forward.

It's not just you. Many people experience this feeling at some point in their lives. It's like the honeymoon phase of a marriage. It starts exciting and new, but eventually, it plateaus, leaving you wondering what's next.

For some people, the highlight of their life is avoiding marriage and family altogether. And that's success for them. They don't want to be tied down, and that's okay. They may have other forms of success, like being a cat mom or dog dad. It's all about finding what success means to you.

But now, you're wondering if you've reached your vision of success. Are you where you want to be? Have you achieved what you set out to do? It's essential to take a step back and assess where you are with your hopes, dreams, and goals.

Early in my life, I had significant successes stacked on top of each other. I graduated high school at sixteen and began working towards a college degree. Even though I had graduated early and could not play school sports, my sports pursuits gained enough notoriety. Some high-level schools recruited me, and ultimately, I was offered a couple of scholarships. I didn't end up going to those universities initially because I was in a garage band at that time, which ended up making two rock albums and started to gain traction.

I was also creating my first company as a digital designer. I was making huge gains with new clients and was only a teenager. Even more, because of my work ethic and attitude, my daytime job wanted me to become a manager at one of their other stores in a different state.

All of that crashed when the September 11th, 2001, attacks took place. From that moment, I canceled all my hopes and dreams and joined the United States Marine Corps as an infantryman. Even in the Marine Corps, I excelled in certain areas, and though I encountered much devastation and loss, my career on paper was a success.

Upon leaving the Marine Corps, I regained my original footing with my digital design company, which skyrocketed immediately after turning it into a media development company to include front-end and back-end web development. I touched briefly on that with the investment from that major company that needed my intellectual property for a Super Bowl advertisement. I excelled, and adding web development pushed me to heights I had never seen in my career. I became an expert at copying and pasting code from the internet! That's a web development joke; moving on.

Not only did my company come back and explode, but sports came back too. I was again offered scholarships to play baseball and football – a major league scout even approached me about playing professionally. However, a significant injury in the Marine Corps prevented this once I took my physical exams for each school and scout.

I was still recovering from a couple of surgeries and ultimately moved into coaching, where I went from one-on-one drills to a head college baseball coach in almost no time. I was one of the top recruiters in the country during this time.

From there, I had one of my videos picked up from social media and turned into a television show I was asked to host. I took that and became an actor and worked on commercials. That allowed me to train at a major studio to become a director. I achieved great heights in my career.

It seemed like everything I touched turned to gold. Yet, I sat in a room and thought that the rest of my life could never compete with this. I have peaked. I stalled and removed myself from the public. I disappeared. I was on my plateau.

The suffering I experienced from this plateau took every attachment from all those successes and placed it in front of me like a lawyer calling me guilty. This lawyer in my mind was screaming at me, "Look how good you were, but now you can't do any of this!" I was attached to all of those titles.

They were essentially "me." Yet, none of them brought me peace; they only brought me more titles. I had a giant trophy room of successes that only made it awkward for me to have everyday conversations with people. I was so wrapped up in my titles that I couldn't see myself. My suffering was found in attachments to titles, and my emotions changed from positive to negative because my titles made my life more difficult, not easier.

You have your vision of success; are you getting there, or did you plateau?

QUESTION THREE

Do you find it hard to be happy and even harder to stay happy? You get good news, but then you're waiting for the other shoe to drop. Think about a time when you were happy, but shortly after, your happiness was overtaken by one of those negative emotions. Do you find yourself waiting for the other shoe to drop?

My dad would say, "sometimes we find out a blessing was needed for a crisis." So, I got a financial blessing and thought of everything I could buy with it. I could invest it into a business or go wild and buy everything in my Amazon cart. But then, something would break. That entire blessing would be gone instantly.

I was once a traveling salesperson for a large regional company. I worked closely with a gentleman who started at the same time I did. We both took off quickly and became very successful in this company.

He and I were in close competition for our company's top two sales positions, which consisted of almost one hundred salespeople. We were thrilled when we were notified that we had reached our bonus targets in sales, which provided us with an added financial boost on top of our commission.

The bonus was significant enough to cover all of my family's bills for the month.

We worked on a 100% commission basis without any salaries or health benefits, so any extra income was a welcome relief. So, we were ecstatic when we received the notification that we both achieved the bonus mark.

Our boss was a negative person who created a negative vibe in the office. So, the culture in the salesroom was toxic and negative. A sense of doom loomed over us when this blessing happened. We were waiting for that other shoe to drop, and it did.

That same day, my friend got a call that his daughter had an accident at school. It wasn't life-threatening, but she was going to need emergency surgery.

We had no benefits, and at this time, we did not have health insurance for our positions. So, this surgery would be entirely out of his pocket.

Can you guess the cost of the surgery? It was almost the amount of the bonus received. My friend was shocked. It was truly peculiar that he received the exact amount needed for his daughter's emergency surgery on the same day.

Instances like that nurture the negative thought of waiting for the other shoe to drop. Have you ever felt like that?

QUESTION FOUR

Do you get frustrated faster than you get excited? Take that earlier shoe when it drops, then after it drops, you'd just assume to stay in the mud. Not only can you not stay excited, but you also roll in the mud for months.

You may even come to a point where you reject good things because all that's going to happen is you'll rise, then the other shoe will drop, and you'll be back in the mud anyway, so why bother? Why be excited? Does the frustration eventually become comfort?

Entrepreneurs don't usually tell you about their failures; they typically post their highlights. Do you follow business leaders on social media? They always have the answers on how to handle objections in sales or how to manage people. They often seem like they've never gotten it wrong. But you know, sometimes they get it wrong. Sometimes you get it wrong. Sometimes I get it wrong. I'm not all highlights.

I created a process to dig a company out of 7 million dollars of debt. I was given one year to carry out this task, but I completed it in 2 months. That's a tremendous highlight, but I haven't been able to do that in every single task

I've ever taken on; I have failures. I had a colossal failure in one of my businesses.

I owned a company, and we teamed up with a separate company on a project. That other company was making money hand-over-fist, and I wanted in on the action.

We didn't know that multiple government agencies were investigating that company. They looked so hard at them that my company became part of the investigation. One of the people working in my building turned out to be an undercover agent. It seemed like that company had a whole government wing coming after them. I put my company in the line of fire, and I didn't even know it.

That other company owner wanted me to send over the money we owed them in cash instead of something trackable. I refused, paid by check, and severed business with them immediately, but it was too late.

They were so entangled that eight businesses associated with them were frozen during the investigation just so the investigators could keep everything contained, which is precisely what happened to us. We had to suspend operations immediately, nothing in, nothing out.

I knew we hadn't done anything wrong, so I figured we would quickly be out of the freeze. We hemorrhaged as the investigation took months. I did whatever I could to reassure people that we would be back as soon as possible. But I also couldn't speak publicly or privately about what was happening, even to close friends or family.

These organizations watched every second of communication coming in or out of that other company, including communication inside my company. Anyone I talked to about it was placed in the investigation.

This was a seriously stressful situation. It went well into the following year, and I was forced to lay off everyone.

Ultimately the other company was shut down, and the rest of us, since we weren't part of their illegal activity, were allowed to resume operation. But I couldn't keep the doors open.

We were gutted and ruined. It killed my business and shut us down completely. I know this is an anomaly, but I should have had my company more prepared for this catastrophe.

For more than a year following this, I constantly received lawsuits. It was a continual flow of people coming after the business and me personally. I couldn't breathe. I was paying for someone else's mistake, but I couldn't help but feel it was all my fault.

I finally just let go. The frustration was so intense that I stopped fighting even though I had defeated every one of those government agencies along the way. Every time I won, I would wake up to another fight and be back in the mud. I found comfort in the mud. I loved the mud more than any comfort I found in temporary success.

My suffering resulted from my attachment to my company, which had now been separated from my sense of self. I could no longer identify with something I had built from a dream. I felt almost every negative emotion on the spectrum time.

However, a closer look would reveal that envy was the emotion that caused me to get involved with that other company. I had seen their success and wanted that same or a higher level of success.

Had I not been envious, I would have never suffered the separation of my company from my "self," nor would shame, guilt, anger, sadness, fear, contempt, or any of the other negative emotions have rushed me so profoundly. Can you see how my need for "self" led to many of my problems in that story?

In your life or business, you have had an instance where you suffer in the mud. Does someone at home or work cause suffering?

Is the mud safer than healing? Staying frustrated is easier than the roller coaster. Have you said that to yourself? Is it easier to be frustrated than excited? What attachment to "self" is involved in your story, and what emotions are driving it?

QUESTION FIVE

Are you beginning to self-destruct? You do things to tear down your body, mind, or soul. It can be substance abuse or any type of addiction.

Close your eyes and have this moment of truth to yourself. Just my voice and your mind. Are you beginning to self-destruct? Is it alcohol? Is it drugs? Is it something else? Is it self-abuse?

You know, when it goes wrong, when that shoe drops, when you find comfort in the mud when you say to yourself that you deserve it when it goes wrong, you're bad, so why not fuel the hate? Do you ever think that to yourself? And so, you self-destruct.

Think of the humor you use. Has someone ever told a joke about you, and it hurts? You know, sometimes you may decide the alternative to that is to tell jokes about yourself and instead direct all insults inward. If you were bullied in school like I was, you might refer to this as beating them to the punch. If you do it first, others won't be able to.

It's called self-deprecating humor. It can be looked upon as very funny in the comedic world. Take your weakness and add a punchline. Everybody laughs. It's just like alcohol. Is one beer terrible? Possibly, but drink 30 beers a night. It's probably not great for you.

If you say one bad thing about yourself, is it wrong? There's an argument in there somewhere. But if you say 30 things back-to-back about yourself that tear you down, that is bad for you because you believe what you are saying about yourself.

It's no longer funny. You are a comedy born of tragedy; the only thing funny about you is how tragic you are - and that's not funny at all, is it? Sometimes people put you there. Sometimes you put your mind there all by yourself. If you're repeatedly told something in your home life, you've been mentally and emotionally abused; you'd better believe it makes it into your work. Maybe your parents or someone growing up did this.

It's impossible not to rise up in all sections of life you have not dealt with. If you're a boss who says, leave home at home and work at work, if it's happening at home, it comes to work, and if it happens at work, it comes home.

You only need to look at self-concept and self-schema to understand this! Your self-concept and self-schema continue even after you change locations. Self-concept is your sense of "self." I'll talk more in-depth about self-concept and self-schema here shortly, so hold this thought.

It comes to work with you because you believe it, so when your tasks don't go well at work, you think you're worthless since you've been told you're worthless. And if you beat them to the punch and self-deprecate. It comes home, and it comes to work. It becomes you.

Self-deprecating humor can be a way for people to cope with difficult situations or negative experiences. However, it is crucial to be mindful of how self-deprecating humor is used and not let it become a negative coping mechanism. Using self-deprecating humor excessively or in a way that harms your self-esteem can be damaging and unhealthy. Finding healthy ways to cope with difficult experiences and build self-confidence and self-worth is essential.

Even beyond humor, sometimes people simply talk terribly about themselves. These same principles apply to this as well. Self-compassion is a powerful tool in your belt; use it.

That self-deprecation may turn into substances. Perhaps you have both. Maybe you have another one I haven't mentioned. Are you doing that? What stories came up in your mind, and what attachments to your "self" came with them? If it's alcohol, did you think about your favorite beer or how you enjoy drinking during social events?

Are there any emotions attached to that situation? What about self-deprecation? Do you insult yourself because of a situation where you feel guilt or shame?

Think about those attachments and emotions. Now, think about those five questions. Do you struggle to do the right thing and still see negative outcomes? Have you hit a plateau in your life and career despite past success? Do you find it challenging to be happy or maintain happiness? Do you get frustrated quickly and have self-destructive behavior? If any sound familiar to you, consider your thoughts in response.

If you don't relate to these experiences, someone around you likely does. It's essential to be equipped to deal with these situations as they may arise in your work or personal life. The goal of asking these questions is to uncover the sources of your suffering.

If these questions don't hit close to home, take time to reflect and identify the root of your pain. It could be something as severe as abuse or a traumatic experience or as seemingly minor as disappointment in a sports team.

No matter the source, it's essential to name and understand your suffering to overcome it. Have that brazen audacity to win and confront it head-on. By doing so, you'll realize that the suffering you've experienced is not as powerful as it may seem. You can defeat it. I've been where you are, and I understand.

CHAPTER 8

Who and What Are You?

You identify yourself by your attachments. These attachments include your body, emotions, personality, thoughts, actions, social roles, and relationships. Your positive and negative beliefs about these elements contribute to your self-concept. However, if someone challenges you or you want to change these beliefs, it requires a shift in your self-concept. You will now explore this to form a more positive self-image and change negative perspectives.

The way you view yourself, known as self-concept, is composed of your beliefs, attitudes, and perceptions about yourself. Your self-concept can change over time as you gain new experiences and information about yourself, like self-perceptions and others' views of you. To process information, your self-concept uses a mental framework called self-schema. Self-schema is a roadmap in your mind leading to your self-concept.

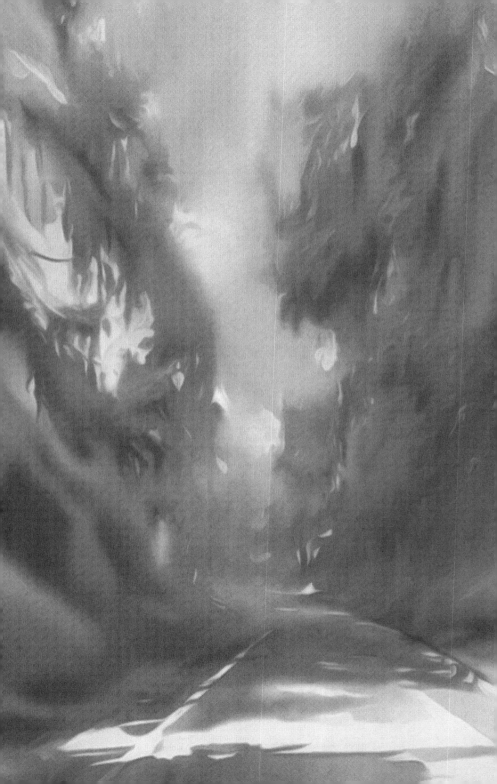

Your self-concept and self-schema significantly shape your decisions, including why you chose to read this message. When you identify with a certain group, like being a veteran or a Christian, your self-concept and self-schema are shaped by those values, beliefs, and behaviors. This can influence your behavior and decision-making.

Next time you make a decision, consider how your self-concept and self-schema may impact your actions. If your self-concept and self-schema are fundamental to you and affect your decision-making, it can lead to suffering because your self-concept has a strong urge to maintain or advance its status quo. Any deviation from this is perceived as an attack or suffering.

So, suppose you opened this writing because you think I am a veteran, a certain political leaning, a man, or anything else you perceive. In that case, those attachments are driving from the home of your self-concept using the road of your self-schema. You then cross the bridge to the road of my self-schema, then arrive at the home of my self-concept.

You will probably be disappointed to discover that my home has no sign in the yard. I do not place attachments on myself and choose none of the attachments you chose for me. I have to work hard at not putting a sign in my yard. Every once in a while, one slips past me, but I remain diligent on this path.

There is a particular reason why I try not to place attachments on you or me. When I entered that door, I saw many things. I saw something that amazed me and things I could not explain. I saw why we are to love one another. I didn't see a famous quote; I saw the actual reason. What I saw was indescribable.

After seeing this, I understand now that any label I place on you devalues the truth of you. I see you beyond any description that you could give yourself. While I respect what you think you are based on your self-concept, if you could see the truth, you, too, would throw the sign out of your yard and live in this indescribable awareness.

The idea that I don't have a sign in my yard could be a small instance of suffering for you because you believe our self-schemas would bridge and our self-concepts may mirror.

Remember, I told you I am not the whole, and neither are you. You are part of the whole, as I am. I cannot escape the truth of what that means, but the expanse of the truth is insulted by any attempt to define it, you, or me, in human words.

Sufferings come from the tension between reality and your self-concept. Your self-concept requires a status quo or advancement. Anything else it calls suffering. Your self-concept makes you aware of your suffering by drawing pictures of the past, pictures in the present, or pictures of the future and then attaching emotions to each. Your self-concept begs you to pay attention to its pictures like a five-year-old with a new box of crayons. So, look at them; they are scribbles.

Looking at your self-concept involves being mindful of your thoughts and utilizing this insight to benefit you. Recognizing the negative aspects of your thoughts is a significant achievement.

You may feel threatened when I point out that these attachments lead to suffering. Your attachment to your beliefs may be so strong that even this message comes across as an attack.

Your self-concept may also resist change and turn away due to fear of losing your identity that it has spent years forming. Your self-concept hates the possibility that all those memories in your past, these perceptions in the present, and those anxieties of the future could be negated.

However, it is essential to confront your suffering and its cause by understanding how your self-concept affects your behavior which can lead to more conscious decision-making. Changing your perspective to a new path requires exploring your suffering and changing your thoughts by remapping your mind.

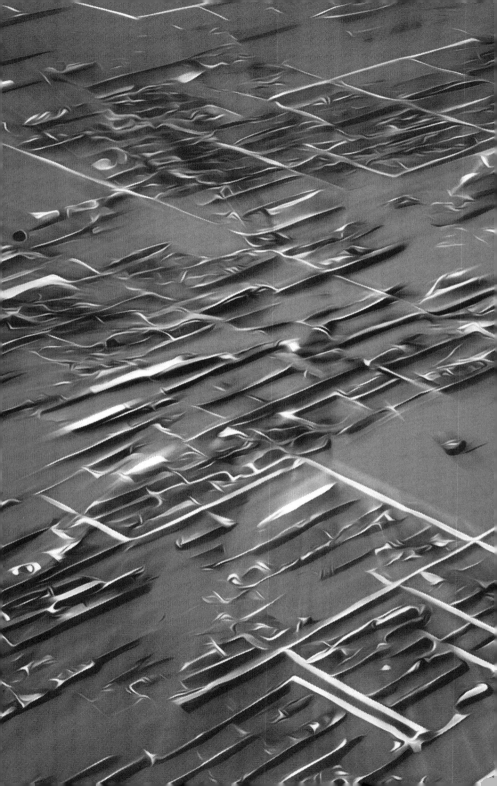

REMAPPING YOURSELF

Remapping your self-schema can bring order and understanding to your self-concept, resulting in greater self-awareness, leading to freedom.

Your mind is a complex and powerful tool. It is responsible for your thoughts, emotions, and behaviors and can perform incredible feats of memory, creativity, and problem-solving. However, this power also comes with great responsibility. A malfunction or shutdown of your mind can result in a complete loss of consciousness and functioning which may not be reversible.

Think of your mind as a city power grid, with the self-schema as the power lines running throughout the city. Just as a city's power grid is responsible for powering and keeping the city running, the self-schema is accountable for carrying information and shaping your self-concept. A breakdown in the power grid can result in an inconvenience, but a breakdown in the self-schema can disrupt our sense of self and identity.

You are going to identify as to what you identify. Then, you will reframe some of those things and possibly wholly remove others. For me, there were three major things I needed to remap. The first was my Marine Corps veteran status. While it can be fun at times, being in the veteran community has grown incredibly toxic and leaning towards venomously negative. Many people stopped identifying as a veteran for this reason.

Another thing I needed to do was remove sports. I grew so strongly identified with sports that I had superstitions that bled into day-to-day activities and family events. If my team lost, I sulked and became irritable, which would cause a snowball effect that never seemed to stop.

A third thing that I needed to remove was social media. Every post on my timeline was either insulting someone, gossiping about another, hating someone, or just general negativity. I removed it.

My decision to remove those three elements from my self-concept wasn't necessarily about individual people because there are people inside those communities that I love and enjoy, but it was because I needed to monitor how much negativity I allowed inside my mind. Unfortunately for those communities, they have, for the most part, chosen the roadmaps of negativity collectively.

All society follows these same roadmaps. You and I have self-concept and self-schema, but groups can also have a collective self-concept and self-schema. This is why groups have infighting constantly. The collective cannot provide a constant match to each individual, resulting in collective suffering, which then trickles down into individual suffering. The individual suffering then recycles itself back to the top of the chain to compound the suffering. Without upkeep, groups tend to become miserable or alienated quickly.

I needed to heal my mind, and those three groups stood in the way. Despite how important the Marines, sports, and social media may be to you, to me, they were my "demons" in disguise.

Eventually, I could view those three things from a new, healthy perspective. They are no longer identities to me, only parts of my story. But I had to remove them for a long time to heal.

What things in your self-concept stand in the way of healing? Are there identities on the individual level or attachments on the collective?

Remapping is a powerful avenue, but it takes time. It's important to remember that remapping self-schema and identifying your self-concept is not a one-time process. Remapping is a lifelong journey of self-discovery and self-improvement.

It's not always easy, but it's essential to be open to new perspectives and to be willing to challenge and change your understanding of your self-concept and self-schema.

To know your self-concept, you must first identify all the voices in your head that attach to those identities in your mind through the intricate structure of your self-schema.

FROM THE VILLAGE TO THE CITY

To paraphrase Aristotle, "What is great in the sphere of a village is small in the sphere of a city." Such is your mind. What once caused great chaos in your mind when its roadmap was small has almost no effect when expanded. Everything I am writing to you about is increasing your cognitive roadmap and lessening the impact of attacks on your mind.

Meditation and mindfulness practices have been shown to positively impact how you process information and navigate any direction of your focus. One of the key benefits of these practices is the ability to increase your cognitive map or the mental model of how the world works.

By developing a deeper understanding of the interconnectedness of things and a greater awareness of your thoughts and emotions, you can learn to respond to individual or group situations more effectively and adaptively.

Events that once caused chaos and confusion can now have little effect when you can navigate any direction of your focus from a broader perspective. You are better equipped to understand the situation's context and see the bigger picture, which can be especially beneficial in a high-stress workplace or personal relationships.

Learning to respond to concerns calmly and measuredly can reduce stress's impact on your life and help you make better decisions. I touched on this briefly when I mentioned that after my event in the garage and during the recovery, I had more circuits and breakers than I had before the drop. Initially, I had no idea how to process the new flow of information. It felt like a character in one of those movies where I could hear and feel everything all at once.

Meditation and mindfulness practices can also help to increase your emotional intelligence. When you are more aware of your own emotions and the emotions of others, you are better able to navigate social interactions and build stronger relationships. This is especially beneficial in the workplace, where strong relationships and effective communication are crucial to success.

Meditation and mindfulness practices can significantly impact how you process information. By increasing your cognitive map and developing a deeper understanding of things, you can learn to respond to situations more effectively.

This can lead to a reduction in stress and an increase in emotional intelligence and empathy, resulting in a more fulfilling and successful life. You can see the benefits of expanding the roadmap of your mind, can't you?

WHOSE RESPONSIBILITY IS THIS?

If you have admitted your suffering and its source, do you believe you can end it? You have called it out to battle. Can you win? I won. You can win. Believe that you can win. To win, first, accept your role in the battle. Here is a picture of how this may look.

A business owner was struggling to keep their company afloat. The owner has a top executive who makes all the company's tough decisions. The owner does not always agree with this executive but rarely interferes with the decisions.

The executive has repeatedly made poor decisions that hurt the company. Yet, because this executive has been at this company for so long, the owner can't find the courage to confront the executive. The attitudes of the management below this executive are all over the map. The dysfunction goes all the way down to the staff.

The staff is belligerent to management. Management is disconnected from the executive, and the executive has overrun the owner's authority. The owner is losing it all.

What you have just done is expose the corporate structure of your mind. Now, if you just watched that whole story unfold in your mind, which one of these people are you?

The executive is your self-concept. It's the one that's always making decisions. It's given various choices by management. Management received the information about those choices by communicating with the staff. That process is your self-schema. But who is at fault for the company's suffering? The executive, management, the staff, or is it the owner?

The owner is responsible for the result of the poor choices but also responsible for the recovery from the suffering. You are the owner and responsible for all your choices, emotions, and suffering. So, it just makes sense to know more about what's going on in the boardroom of your mind, doesn't it?

If you're approaching this from a faith perspective, you might be upset when I talk about the executive being your self-concept because you have the attachment that your faith is the driving force. You and I are saying the same thing.

Your attachment to your faith is integral to your self-concept and self-schema, influencing your decision-making. You form your faith principles by incorporating teachings, scripture, and texts through reading and prayer, which adds to your self-concept.

This is not a removal of God but rather a heightened awareness of God through the proper use of your mind. The aim is to show you the enemy, not take away God.

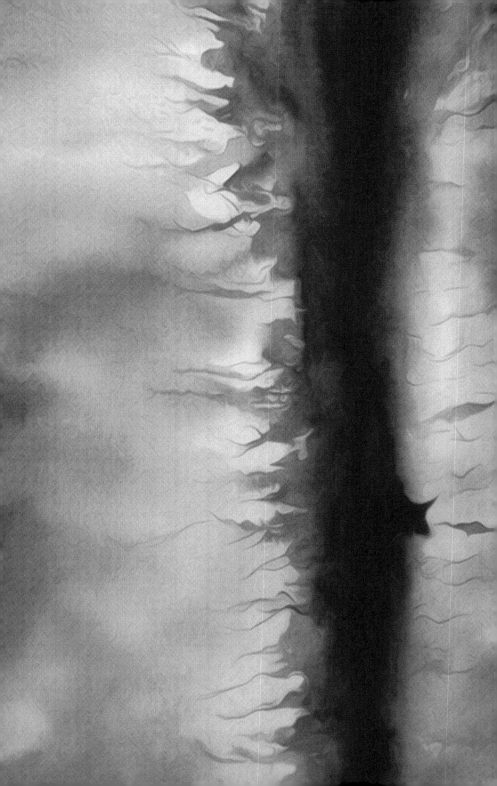

CHAPTER 9

Sharpening Your Skills

Look at how far you've come in such a short time. You want to make your life better because it's no longer about whether I believe you can do it; it's because you're starting to believe that you can do it too. It's because you can. I am about to walk you through some of the tips and techniques I use for keynote speaking engagements, workshops, and sports counseling, so if you enjoy them and want me to walk your company, organization, or team through these and many others, please reach out.

Let's go to the gym. You could build your mind gym metaphorically. The gym, in your mind, allows you to work out anytime you want. You don't have to stay in the gym either. You can also roam the halls and pick other rooms in your mind. You can have various machines for exercising and strengthening different functions of your mind.

Your brain constantly adapts and changes in response to your experiences and environment. This process, known as neuroplasticity, allows your brain to learn and grow throughout your life continually. By engaging in activities that challenge and stimulate your brain, you can help maintain and improve its function.

The next time someone tells you about their gains from the gym, you can tell them about your gains due to the neuroplasticity of your mind and your mental gym. They may even ask you what you are talking about, and you'll get to put one more person on track to solving problems in their mind. Unless you thought this was a secret to keep to yourself for your advantage? It's not; this is not your secret weapon to hide.

Taking care of your overall physical health is also essential, so the people from the gym need to know this stuff too. Just remember, you can only bring someone to the door.

Your physical health can have a significant impact on your brain functions. Moreover, getting enough sleep, physically exercising regularly, eating a healthy diet, and managing stress play an essential role in your mental health.

Taking care of your brain and body can help maintain and improve your function and well-being. Doing mental exercises continually strengthens your ability to control your emotions, memories, and, ultimately, you. At first, you may not be very good at any of this, but over time you will be a heavy lifter and able to move about in your mind easily.

Neuroplasticity, which I touched on briefly earlier, can occur at any stage of life. It can also involve brain structure, function, and connectivity changes. Neuroplasticity is a powerful construct.

Neuroplasticity allows your brain to learn and adapt continually. It is thought to play a role in learning, memory, and recovery from brain injuries. It is also believed to be a key mechanism underlying your brain's ability to compensate for damage or dysfunction, such as stroke or degenerative diseases like Alzheimer's.

The construct of neuroplasticity has deepened the understanding of the human brain and has led to new treatments and therapies for various neurological and psychiatric conditions. Neuroplasticity is the "gains" from working out or exercising your brain.

Bring your focus back to the battlefield against your suffering. Who are you if you called your attachments and your suffering out to the battlefield? You see the battlefield, yet no camera shows you? All the things that the self-schema says you are out there. Yet, you see them. Who and what are you?

THE MOVIES OF YOUR MIND

I am a place where thoughts and feelings reside.
A place where the past and present collide.
I can be a source of inspiration or a source of
doubt.
I can lift you up, or I can drag you down.
I am the home of your dreams and your fears.
I can be far away and also near
What am I?

If you answer the riddle correctly, you answer your "self" incorrectly because you may not know yourself as well as you think you do. Grasp the spirit of the riddle and the soul of the answer.

You will start this section with a simple step-by-step walkthrough. You just went over the meditation section of this writing. I will reintroduce a portion of that here to get this next session started. Be ready for battle. So, get comfortable and relax. Here is your walkthrough:

Find a quiet and comfortable space where you can sit or lie down undisturbed. Sit or lie down comfortably, keeping your back straight, and your body relaxed. Close your eyes.

Take a few deep breaths. Relax, close your eyes, and slowly breathe in through your nose until your lungs are full. Hold your breath for a second, and then slowly breathe out through your mouth. Pay attention to how the air feels as it moves in and out of your body.

Quietly in your mind, ask yourself, "what am I?" Take one more deep breath in while you count to four, out while you count to six at an even yet easy pace. You may do this multiple times if you want to. Pay attention to how the air feels as it moves in and out of your body while you breathe.

Focus on the sensation of the air entering and leaving your body. Breathe in and count slowly to four. Let it out and count slowly to six. Bring your attention to your breath. Do this as often as you need to until you start calming down.

Focus on the breath's sensation as it enters and leaves your nose or mouth. If your mind starts to wander, gently bring your attention back to your breath. Don't judge yourself for getting lost in your thoughts. It's natural to do so. If your thoughts wander, recognize them and return to your breath.

Allow your breath to return to its natural pattern. I want you to envision an oversized home theater chair in your home. It's a large comfortable recliner, and in front of it is a giant screen. Can you imagine that? You're holding the camera watching this. Your eyes are the camera. On the screen, you have various movies from which to select.

Before you choose one, make sure you see out past the recliner and onto the screen with all the movies from which to select. Feet lifted on the recliner. The arm holding the remote, resting comfortably on the armrest. Can you envision that?

Look at one of those movies and place a picture representing a memory that may be what you think you are. Can you envision that? What do you see? Please give it a title. You see the picture of the memory, lay a title overtop.

It can be what you tell people that you are. Make that movie appear on the screen. Move to another movie. Slide over to the next one and create that picture the same way you created the first one. What is another thing that you tell people that you are? Please give it a title. You can do as many as you want. Keep going if you want to. Can you envision it?

Look past the reclined feet and at the screen at your selection of movies. Now, as the camera's eyes move back slowly to see everything from behind your chair, move the eyes of the camera. Looking over the chair, the shoulder, the arm with the remote, past the recliner feet, and onto the screen with the movies and their titles. Can you envision that? I want you to calmly reach up to the arm of the chair and take the remote. It's your remote.

Create a new movie about a crowd circling one person. Who is the one person they are circling? Is it you? Let's make the person you. But I want you to look like you do right now. Whatever you're wearing is what the "you" character has on in this movie. Select this movie.

It opens, and you see the crowd circling this one person. This person who is you and looks like you, wearing what you're wearing. The mass of people can even represent people from your memories, old or new, who may have been negative in some way to you.

The title comes across the screen. The movie is called "What Am I?" The title layers over the view of this crowd and this one person, who is "you." I'm going to describe the people in the crowd now. You have:

Ten, telling you no.
Nine, telling you to go.
Eight, breaking your heart.
Seven, tearing your dream apart.
Six, stealing your light.
Five, taking your sight.
Four, taking your heart.
Three, hating you from the start.
Two, mocking everything you do.
One is the same as you.
Then there is you, with the crowd in your eyes.
You are...

Then before you can see the answer to what you are, the movie begins to zoom in on the "you" character and, as it gets closer to it, gains momentum starting from above the crowd. It speeds up, and then you see the eyes of the "you" character from a few feet away as it speeds. It zips past the crowd and directly into the retina of the "you." Then the screen fades to black as the movie is set to begin. Watch the screen fade to black.

Sit here in the black for a moment. Take a deep breath. Let it out slowly. Slowly come back to now. Open your eyes if they are closed. Take notice of how you feel.

The technique used here is a form of guided imagery meditation. You were looking into your awareness or metacognition. Did you see how you could jump from one movie to the other? You took inventory of your memories and emotions and could see many different thoughts and emotions.

Some may seem harmless, and that is because suffering is dormant until it becomes what you know as suffering. Part of defeating suffering is beating it before, while, and after it is suffering. So, the harmless ones only lack the variable of time.

Your mind has told you that it was in charge of you your entire life. But if you could look at the emotions in your mind and pick between memories, who showed you those memories? It wasn't me, and it wasn't you because you were behind the chair watching it all. You had the remote, but you didn't paint those pictures. Your mind did that for you. They only existed once they were spoken into existence. Such is your suffering.

In the riddle, you answered "mind," but you just watched your mind work, so you are not your mind. What are you?

In the corporate structure of your mind, one of your managers brought the executive a series of images. The manager received those images from a coordinated effort in your mental structure. One staffer sent an image of a crowd to a manager. A second sent an image of you, while another sent the image of the room where this took place. Your mind worked as a team to provide the management with the images, who then gave the final product to the executive. Except for this time, you were watching it all happen.

But how long have you assumed you were the executive - the one in the chair, the one with the remote? You have never been the one in the chair. You are the owner.

Your mind team helped you during those life events then, which your mind turned to pictures now. Your mind presented you with a choice of emotions then, and your mind presented you with a selection of emotions now. Your mind has always been doing this. It's doing it now, and it will continue to do so.

However, now you know this, you have no excuse for the "devil made me do it" or the "I'm always grumpy, it's just me" stuff. That type of thinking is proven false. Your mind is not "you."

Your mind is your corporation that runs the "you." You are a separate entity joined together with your self-schema and self-concept. If you're angry, you have allowed the executive to choose anger. If you're grumpy, you have let the executive choose contempt. If you're happy, you have allowed the executive to choose happiness for you.

Up until now, you decided by delegation or even unsuspectingly. So, whose fault is your faulty corporation? The real you is to blame because you have let that executive run wild and make careless choices at critical times.

However, today, you are reaching forward and taking back the remote. You have called your self-concept onto the battlefield by naming and viewing your attachments and emotions.

This tactic was precisely how I recovered the images of my children's faces in my mind. I recalled them through this process, and the connection was reset. Now you have this tool at your disposal.

A NOTEWORTHY ACCOMPLISHMENT

Think about what you saw with those images and titles across the screen. Using either a pen and paper or a note-taking app, describe what you saw and felt in the best way you can. It doesn't have to be a fluid story.

Keep that note for yourself as a journal. Do that as often as you are able. The journaling technique is a significant player in cognition and mental health. The most profound healing in your life will often happen at times when you are actively journaling. You don't have to write a book; you could write one line as it comes to you, dive into it right then, or save it for later.

This practice will help with memorization as well as healing. Sometime down the road, you may think you're in a rut, then you read one of your early entries, and you'll see how far you've come. This message you're reading now started as a journal entry that became a larger thought.

Remember in the introduction, I stated that I didn't immediately begin writing this because of circumstances in my life? Well, I was journaling then, so I could look back and see the map of my mind and expand on specific thoughts I had begun to dive into but had not completed.

I even used the movies of my mind exercise to work through traumatic events, such as losing friends to horrific, graphic, and violent deaths. I used it to heal from my painful divorce, and I used it to recover from the extreme trauma of losing the ability to recognize my children in pictures.

The images of their faces were blocked in my mind from the trauma. I used this practice to recover their faces, ultimately mending my shattered heart. I had profound guilt of thinking how mentally bankrupt of a father I must be not to be able to recognize my children's faces. This guilt led to powerful fear.

Fear finds its way into many of your movies. Sometimes because of trauma, sometimes because of self-destruction. Fear will hand you a guilty verdict for past, present and future occurrences. Fear was from a liar, and your mind chooses the title for every movie: fear! But when you move the eyes of your camera back while in that room, you see that your mind is in that chair, not you. Those images are creations of things that happened, but they aren't the definition of "you."

You will find sadness and joy, successes, and failures. I, too, found most of my collection. I used to have a massive collection of movies, and I could take inventory of my sadness and joy:

I'm a Texan, Kansan, and from coastal sand.
I even once called my home Iceland,
I've been a musician, I've been a poet,
I've had a tv show that I hosted.
I've been an athlete, then a coach.
I've been recruited and poached.
I've been a Marine, a leader of men
I've had brothers; I buried some of them.

I've been a reader, I've been an author.
A husband and a father.
I've been married., I've been divorced.
I've been remarried, of course.
A graphic designer, and even a pastor.
A content creator and an actor.
I've been a spokesperson, a silent partner.
I've been peaceful, and I've been a fire starter.

I've been a sports fan, I've been a sports agent.
I've been a director of public relations.
I've owned a business, and I've been a janitor
I've been entry-level, and I've been a manager.
I've been a salesman, a sales director.
I've been in just about every sector,
I've won, and I've suffered defeat.
I've been on stage, and I've lost my seat.
I, too, found myself in that crowd,
The camera looking down.

Ten who told me no,
Nine who told me to go.
Eight who broke my heart,
Seven who tore my dream apart.
Six who stole my light,
Five who took my sight.
Four who took my heart,
Three who hated me from the start.
Two who mocked everything about my life,
One who was the same as I.
There was "me," with the crowd in my eyes,
What am I?

What you just tapped into in your mind is metacognition. Quick reminder, metacognition means being aware of your awareness. While being aware of your awareness is one step, it's time to work once you've become aware.

So, enter the boardroom of your mind. Being aware of your thoughts means you can control and manage them. This powerful tool makes you more efficient and effective with your thought processes. You are now in charge, the real "you," not your self-concept. Now you can name the emotion and the story, then decide what needs to happen with it. You choose.

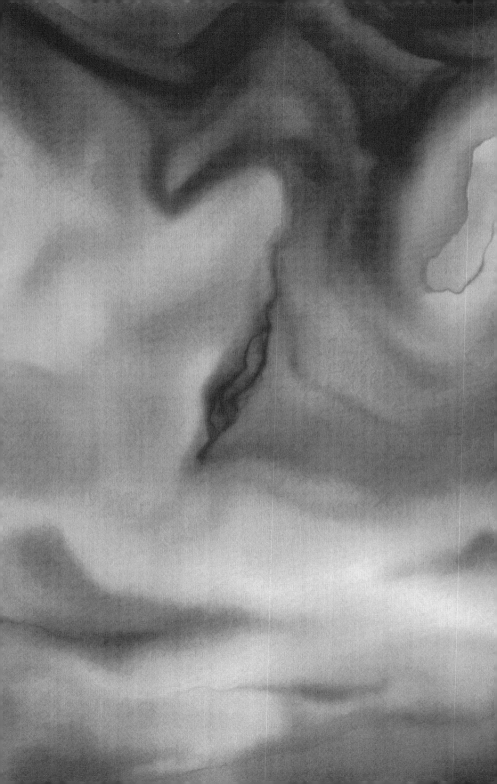

NAME IT TAME IT

Another tool for calling out your emotions is the "Name it, Tame it" method. It is a simple yet effective technique for managing difficult emotions. Dr. Dan Siegel, a clinical professor of psychiatry at the UCLA School of Medicine, developed this method based on the idea that giving an emotion's name can help decrease its intensity and make it more manageable.

The first step in using the "Name it, Tame it" method is to become aware of the emotion you are experiencing. You may have to pause for a moment and focus on your physical sensations, such as a racing heart or tightness in the chest.

Once you have identified the emotion, name it by simply stating it aloud or quietly under your breath. Think about those movies that came across the screen. The next time you do that exercise, name the emotion the movie has attributed to it.

By naming the emotion, you are bringing it into conscious awareness, which can help to decrease its intensity. Labeling the emotion creates a separation between you and the emotion, making it less overwhelming and more manageable. This is the Taming part. Acknowledging your emotions and seeing them for what they are is essential.

Using the "Name, it Tame it" method, you can learn to become more aware of your emotions and develop the skills to manage them more effectively.

The "Name it, Tame it" method is not only to name and tame the emotions but to take a step further and reflect on what triggered that particular emotion. Then find how it might connect to a more profound unmet need or an unresolved past event.

This can help you to understand yourself better, which can provide valuable insight and can help with emotional regulation and healing.

The "Name it, Tame it" method is a simple yet effective technique for managing difficult emotions. Becoming aware of the emotion through reaction to an event or by metacognition, then giving it a name, decreases its intensity and makes it more manageable. This can help you to develop a deeper understanding of yourself and to learn to manage emotions more effectively.

You just walked through a process of calling out your suffering and naming it. Then once it's named, its effects become limited, mainly because its primary source of pain is in its attachment to you. Once you make it admit that it is indeed not you, it no longer has its weapon. This practice takes time, and you will need to do this repeatedly. There is no limit. So, keep working on these principles until you master them.

TAKE THE EASY WINS

Easy wins along the way can greatly impact your motivation and momentum. These wins don't have to be big and grand but rather simple daily habits that you can easily incorporate into your life. Celebrating easy wins boosts your confidence and motivation, providing a sense of accomplishment.

These wins are for that moment and should not be viewed as a measure of your life's success or failure. Keeping a score will only lead to disappointment and frustration when you miss a day, and you will miss a day, and that's okay. Focus on enjoying each win in the moment and enjoy the boost in confidence and motivation.

These wins are just for the moment and should not define your success or failure. Focus on enjoying each win as it comes and savor the boost in confidence and motivation that comes with it.

The following is not a comprehensive or the ultimate list; they're just simple things. You may even have something you would like to add to the list. It doesn't matter as long as it's easy for you to accomplish daily.

With this in mind, here are a few to focus on that can serve as easy wins in your journey. So, take a deep breath and get ready to celebrate the small wins that come with each task you complete.

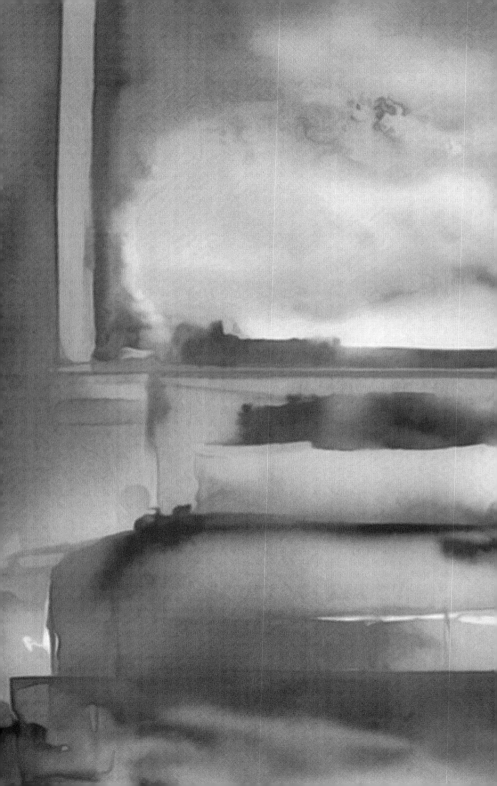

You Made Your Bed. Now You Must Lie in It.

A simple thing you can do in the morning is making the bed. It's not crazy, and it's not outlandish; it's simple. Make the bed for one easy win before you even have your coffee. It's small, but the small steps are the winning steps because most people aren't willing to take them.

If you're like me, you aren't a massive fan of doing this. So, I found a hack for me, and you can use it too. I went to the store and bought sheet clasps, and then I clasped the bottom portion of the flat sheet at both corners with diagonal clips.

So, it stays in place all night, and then in the morning, when it's time to make the bed, pull the sheets and the blanket to the top and throw all 15 of my wife's pillows back on the bed.

This clasp trick has moved the bed-making from 3 minutes to about 15-30 seconds in the morning, and the bed looks and feels way better with secured sheets. Stealing an easy win and doing it quickly is a solid start to the day, isn't it?

Don't worry; I clasp the sheet far enough back to still be able to stick my foot out over the side of the bed like normal people. This practice is simple, but it positively affects my emotions at the start of my day, and it is one of the easiest wins you could ever give yourself. Take advantage of it.

The Need for Speed

One of the best things I ever did during this process was I stopped speeding. Despite the obvious legal and safety concerns, one compounding situation I found each day centered around my driving faster than the speed limit.

I know I am taking away the fun right at the beginning of your journey, I get it, but drastic results require drastic measures. Here's how it helped me. Maybe it can help you.

I was getting caught in slower traffic and couldn't pass. My frustration would compound with each vehicle I would find myself stuck behind. The frustration led to mental arguments with other drivers on the road.

By the time I arrived at my office, I was already seven arguments deep into my day, causing my first interaction with anyone in my path to be negative. If they're negative, too, we compounded our frustrations two-fold. My negativity grew for no other reason, and I needed to get to where I was going a couple of minutes sooner.

Stopping my speeding was a symptom of a deeper underlying issue like anger. But slowing down gave me a clearer perspective and avoided unnecessary arguments. It was a simple change, but it made me feel happier and motivated to continue.

Drinking

Drinking water is a simple yet effective way to improve physical and mental health. Consuming sugary drinks hurts your overall health, but drinking water reduces stress.

Drinking water helps lower cortisol levels, reducing stress on the body. By staying hydrated, you can also improve your mood and attitude, and it helps your brain function at its highest capacity.

Next time you're stressed, reach for a water bottle instead of a sugary drink. Not only will you reduce your stress levels, but you will also be doing your overall health a favor. Make drinking water a daily habit and carry a water bottle to ensure you get enough hydration.

Drinking less alcohol also reduces stress levels by lowering the hormone cortisol in your body. This one hit pretty close to home because I spent nearly fifteen years as an alcoholic. Some of my worst moments in life have been because of drinking too much alcohol.

I know this may ruin the party for you when you add more water and remove speeding but consider the cost. You're going through a journey to change your life, and you're not going to be the same at the end as you were at the beginning, which means things might go away.

Get Away from The Office

Getting away from the office seems like a no-brainer to me, but maybe you're a workaholic. Do you stay at the office for hours on end?

Working long hours can lead to high levels of stress and burnout. Getting away from the office can help you get better sleep and help you discover that work-life balance concept you may have heard about. Besides, getting away from the office is sometimes where the real stories happen.

I worked on Capitol Hill in DC for a government relations firm. The job was stressful, so we would have to get away from the office and have some fun around town. I would visit all the city's monuments, historic districts, and even historic diners.

Once, a few of us from the office went to a fancy restaurant in Georgetown. This restaurant was dimly lit to provide an elegant feel. The dim lighting made it difficult to see most of the people dining. It also hid much of the restaurant.

After a while, I needed to step away from our table to use the restroom. When I entered the restroom, a man immediately made eye contact. His face lights up, and then he walks right to me but right by the sink like it doesn't exist. Then he sticks out his hand to shake mine! "Glad to see you back!" He exclaims! I had never eaten here before.

I looked at this man's hand, which never touched soap or water in the sink - the dilemma. I dodged him with the international "ew" position. He looked humiliated. He awkwardly passed by me and proceeded back downstairs. I soon returned to our table to find the man waiting for me, but now he and another person were standing at my table waiting for me! What did I do wrong!? But then both of their faces light up! What is going on!? This man goes in for round two.

He didn't pass a sink on the way here, but he's still trying to get me to shake that hand. I gave him the shimmy and sat down at my table. His face sank low. He was embarrassed. I didn't know what to do. I was confused. At this point, I felt bad for what I did and thought about just shaking his hand to make the man feel better.

This first man had told his friend that I was Zac Brown. I don't see the resemblance, but he did. I never corrected him. So, to this day, there are a couple of people in DC who think Zac Brown doesn't like them. Getting out of the office can help with work-life balance, help you sleep better, and it can write some colorful stories in your life. But please wash your hands.

CHAPTER 10

How You Treat Others

By understanding your emotions and having tools to manage them, it's crucial to apply this knowledge in your interactions with others. Understanding your emotions can enhance your relationships and communication.

I found that my emotions often led to negative behavior and strained relationships. To break this cycle, I applied the techniques I learned to regulate my emotions in everyday situations, resulting in a more positive and constructive approach to interactions as well as improved relationships.

By using your emotional intelligence in a practical way, you can improve your own life and positively impact those around you. Being more aware of your emotions and how they influence your behavior can inspire others to regulate their emotions and improve their relationships.

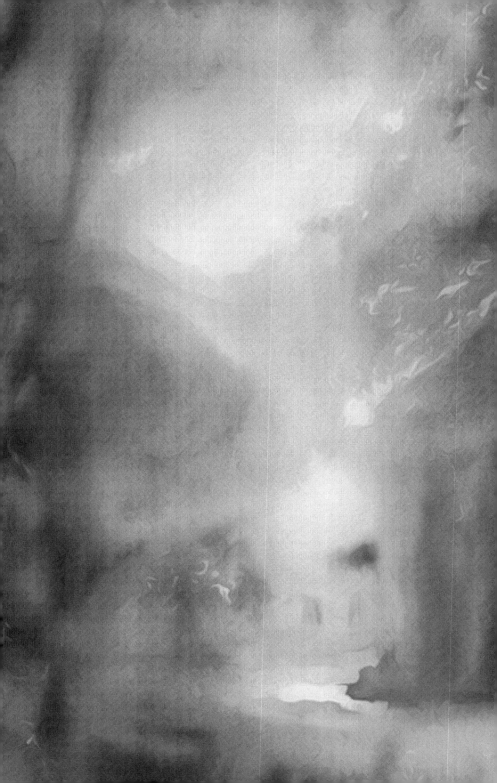

EMOTIONAL INTELLIGENCE

One of my favorite superpowers to use for this is called emotional intelligence. Yes, it's a superpower, and it makes you a superhuman. Meditation and mindfulness are as well. In case I forgot to tell you. Emotional intelligence works amazingly in practical application for you and the person you are dealing with.

Emotional intelligence, or the ability to recognize and manage your own emotions and the emotions of others, has been found to play a significant role in various aspects of life. I figured this one out at just the right time in life. But when I figured it out, I realized how many people from whom I needed to ask for forgiveness. Whereas you now know more about your emotions, emotional intelligence recognizes those same things in others.

Once you become a master of your emotions, then you master emotional intelligence, and you will begin seeing people with a whole new set of eyes. You will see them truer than they even see themselves. It can be unnerving at first because you will begin to realize that the "gut feeling" you once thought was a myth is an actual practice and resides in emotional intelligence.

When my wife was pregnant with our son, she began experiencing a strange phenomenon. She began to have anxiety and depression when she used to be happy and always joking. She was always lively, yet now she was always low. Me having a "tough love" mindset built into me in the Marine Corps as well as in athletics and coaching; I thought this would be the time to pull that card out and use it. I had buried this "tough love" card for many years.

I encouraged her with strong words and negative imagery if she failed. When that didn't work, I got frustrated and resorted to more negativity toward her. I didn't know at the time that she was dealing with the start of "postpartum depression," and it would continue after our son was born.

What I did was exceedingly dangerous for her, the baby, and me. I had no clue. I had only been out of the Marine Corps a short time, and the temperament, though not one I didn't actively use anymore, sometimes worked for me there. It wasn't working here. My wife began to suffer deeply.

My confusion and anger caused me to fight back at her. Neither of us knew that she needed help, and that help would have opened a door for healing for her and me. But we didn't do it. We didn't look for help. We just vented and argued with each other, heaping piles of resentment on each other with each conversation.

We continued to argue to the point that only a few short years later, I found solace from the arguments in that garage. That me, the one from that day, would tell you it was her fault. The me who woke up a few months later from that garage knows the truth.

The truth is that she was depressed, low, and suffering constantly; she was going through something that she physiologically and psychologically could not fight on her own.

I was her helper, her helpmate, in sickness and health, for better or worse, but I became the knife in her back. I became the ice-cold air to a weak lung. I became the wrong person at the wrong time. My reaction to her suffering almost ended me. It did, however, end our marriage not long after. You can see now how that event in the garage didn't actually happen that night in the garage, can't you?

After my first marriage ended in divorce, I found love again and remarried. My new wife and I were overjoyed when we discovered she was pregnant. Despite our happiness, the memories of my first wife's suffering during pregnancy came flooding back. My new wife had experienced several miscarriages, and now, she was showing the same signs of stress and anxiety that I had seen in my past marriage. I was determined not to repeat the mistakes I made the first time.

I told my new wife my experiences and the emotions that came with them and let her know I understood her feelings. I promised to support her through the good and the bad. We talked openly about her anxieties, and that brought her comfort. I told her that this process could continue even after our baby was born. And that I would still be with her during that time. She realized that while not all women experience postpartum depression, those who do often suffer deeply. Together, we would navigate this journey and ensure she was safe and supported.

But how can you improve your emotional intelligence? One way, which I just told you about, is to practice mindfulness. This is how I discovered it. Developing empathy and learning to recognize and manage emotions in yourself and others can also help to improve emotional intelligence.

Emotional intelligence plays a crucial role in your relationships and overall well-being. By practicing mindfulness, developing compassion, and learning to recognize and manage emotions, you can easily improve your emotional intelligence and navigate life.

COMPASSION

You don't have to go far in my story to look at compassion. The earlier story about emotional intelligence required my compassion for my wife. My understanding of my failures in my previous marriage required compassion for my ex-wife.

I remember one particular significant moment when compassion hit home for me. It was the day I sat with my divorce attorney for the first time. It was just a few days after getting the divorce papers from the sheriff's officer in the lobby at work.

For the first few hours after receiving those papers, I was suffering. I thought of all the things I could do to fire back. But I calmed myself with about two straight days of meditation and mindfulness, to which I concluded. That woman is the mother of my children. If I pursue this situation in hate, I teach my children that it's okay to hate their mother.

I soaked in compassion for two days. I focused entirely on why she deserved compassion. After this, I walked into my attorney's office and told her that we would take every punch they threw and never throw a punch back at her. I never want my kids to see me degrade their mother. My attorney was shocked. She said, "nobody ever acts like that; they always try to fight back."

Her attorney attacked me for months. She gutted me and never relented. I was left without a home, and my kids, job, and dogs were gone. I was left with nothing.

I was left wandering without a home. That familiar character I've played before. But this was act two on the stage. Both times looking for someone, one lost, one found, and one more found with each page.

Everyone around me watched me so close during this time. They watched me, and they watched for my old friend – that power without definition. But my friend didn't come back, those overgrown weeds, that damaged field: it was burning into a black sky.

Everyone said it was time to fight, but I never fought back and carried my path of compassion to full term. My mantra was "win with love." After months, they finally relented.

I meditated for eight hours a day, with sessions in the morning, then more at night. That is more than most people would or could meditate, but it was key when I needed peace or a deeper understanding of the situation, allowing me to sink deep into the fight for compassion.

Ultimately, I did win with love. Compassion wins. Everything came back. My ex-wife and I did not get back together, but we became good friends.

She and my current wife are very good friends. My wife even wrote a children's book titled "Just Us" by RaeAnn Childress on Amazon, describing this co-parenting dynamic in an easy-to-read fashion.

My wife's book inspires me because my goal is to explain my entire journey to children. Yet, she's already done that with her enjoyable children's book, which explains the complexity of co-parenting using easy-to-understand language.

The story of our journey to co-parenting was brutal. We won with love, and we fought with compassion. You may not win that way. You may use compassion, and they never stop kicking you. The answer is not the one you're going to want in that situation because the answer is to stay compassionate even if they kick you into the grave. This is the way.

Is this something for which you have had trouble? People can be awful and sometimes go out of their way to hurt you. I'm sure you've spent more than a few minutes on social media, haven't you? That place is brutal.

Compassion is not just being nice; it's looking at the other person when they're hurting and being in that moment with them. As I had deep compassion for my ex-wife, I also have deep compassion for you.

Compassion is a powerful tool that involves feeling concern and empathy for the suffering of others and a desire to help alleviate that suffering. It is closely related to other positive emotions, such as empathy, love, and kindness. It is considered to be an essential aspect of human well-being.

Compassion affects your physical and mental health positively. People who regularly experience compassion have lower levels of stress and inflammation and are more likely to have a positive outlook on life.

Compassion can improve relationships, which can positively impact your overall well-being. Despite these benefits, however, compassion can be challenging to practice. Your natural tendency to focus on your concerns and priorities can make it difficult to feel compassion for others. The overwhelming nature of certain suffering can make it hard to know how to respond or empathize with the situation or person.

In the beginning, I told you that people could use these practices for other than honorable purposes. One of the easiest ways to sniff them out is their lack of genuine compassion. They cannot practice compassion in truth because they are self-seeking and chasing their greed. Your subconscious or gut feeling will quickly detect it. This can also be called discernment from a faith perspective.

Developing compassion requires practice, but it can be strengthened through mindfulness and meditation. By training your attention and awareness, you can become more sensitive to the needs of others and more responsive to their suffering.

Another way is to practice active listening, fully listening and understanding the person's feelings, problems, and ideas. This can help you to understand them better and to be more compassionate towards them. Volunteering, philanthropy, and other acts of kindness can also help you develop compassion.

These activities allow you to connect with others and see firsthand how your actions can impact them. One practical way for compassion to positively impact and reduce stress simultaneously is to be generous. You could buy someone's groceries, fill up their tank, or buy them a cup of coffee. It doesn't have to be a huge gesture but giving to someone else is a practical way to help both you and them.

Compassion is essential to your humanity and something you can strive to cultivate. Doing so can improve your well-being and bring peace to any perspective in any direction of your focus.

After reading about emotional intelligence and your basic emotions, do you see the importance of compassion for others and yourself?

FORGIVENESS

Forgiveness is a difficult bridge to cross, but it's necessary; be prepared to face this challenge. Though it may not make sense now, you will understand when the time comes. It will be frightening but also amazing. You can do this.

Without crossing this bridge, your journey ends here. If you don't cross, your eyes will never see, and your ears will never hear. No exceptions, not even small grudges like "forgive but never forget." You hold no score against another person or yourself. This is why this way is traveled by so few. Most people turn away at this point. Will you?

Forgiveness is a powerful and complex process that can profoundly impact your mental, emotional, and physical well-being. It is the act of letting go of resentment, anger, or other negative feelings toward someone who has hurt you and choosing to move forward with compassion.

The process of forgiveness is not easy; it can take time and effort to truly let go of negative emotions and heal from past hurts. However, the benefits of forgiveness are well worth the effort.

Forgiveness can lead to improved mental health, decreased stress and anxiety, and improved physical health.

Forgiveness starts with comprehending the injury or hurt, analyzing one's role and emotions, and considering the other person's viewpoint and contributing factors.

Once you clearly understand the situation, you can begin to let go of your anger and resentment. This may involve expressing your feelings in a safe and supportive environment, practicing self-compassion, and finding ways to remove negative emotions.

Another significant aspect of forgiveness is empathy. Understanding the human condition of the person who has hurt you can help shift your perspective. In some cases, it's possible to reach out to the person who hurt you to resolve any remaining conflicts and misunderstandings and possibly rebuild.

Forgiveness requires compassion, kindness, and understanding toward the person who has hurt us. It involves viewing them as human rather than villains and acknowledging that they, too, may be on a journey of growth and healing.

Forgiveness is a process that requires time and patience. It is not something that can be rushed or forced. It is critical to be patient with yourself and to remember that healing takes time.

Forgiveness is a powerful tool for healing and growth, and it can profoundly impact your mental, emotional, and physical well-being. While the process of forgiveness can be complicated, the benefits are well worth the effort.

I stood over my best friend's body. They say he's at peace now, but I see pieces missing and an emptiness. It's not fair to be young and already proficient at pain. Why him? But I'm alive? I'm too young to be good at final goodbyes.

As a result of my best friend's death, I developed a lot of hatred toward the person who took his life so violently. I built on the hate which started with all of the previous deaths. He was the sixteenth, and it had been a year since my first friend started it all - sixteen in one year. I hadn't felt anger like this before.

Initially, I lived in anger, but eventually, I decided in my heart to forgive. True forgiveness was the way; it was a gut-wrenching thought because it required total commitment.

You may not have a story of a violent loss. Still, I'm sure you have a time when you were met with profound adversity which eventually left you at odds with someone else. As hard as it may be, this bridge must be crossed, or this journey will end. It may take you time but work towards it. After reading through the positive effects that forgiveness can have on your life, do you now understand the importance of forgiveness to others and yourself?

GRATITUDE

Can you remember a time when you were grateful for something or someone? How did that gratitude make you feel? Identifying and reflecting on things you are grateful for can be a positive way to shift your focus to positive aspects of your life - thus increasing overall well-being and satisfaction.

Gratefulness is the act of feeling or showing appreciation for something that one has received. It is a powerful tool that can significantly impact your well-being and happiness. Practicing gratitude can make you more satisfied with life and better your physical and mental health.

You may notice many of gratitude's positive outcomes, including increased happiness and well-being, improved physical health, and stronger relationships. Practicing gratitude could even help to provide better sleep quality. Sleep would be nice, wouldn't it?

One of the most effective ways to cultivate gratitude is to keep a gratitude journal. This is a simple practice in which one writes down a list of things they are grateful for daily. This can include big things, like a new job or a happy relationship, and small things, like a pleasant sunset or a hot cup of coffee. Regularly reflecting on the things you are grateful for can shift your focus.

Expressing gratitude to others can also help cultivate gratitude. Simply saying "thank you" or showing appreciation for the big and the small things people do for you can strengthen relationships and make both parties feel grateful.

Writing letters of gratitude to people who have positively impacted your life could increase happiness and satisfaction. You can also volunteer or help others to practice gratitude by supporting others who may be less fortunate than you.

Gratitude is a powerful action that can positively impact your well-being and happiness. By cultivating gratitude through practices such as keeping a gratitude journal, practicing mindfulness, and expressing gratitude to others, you can learn to appreciate the things you often take for granted. How can you implement gratitude in your life?

CHAPTER 11

Learning How to Listen

Do you ever wonder why some people navigate life and relationships effortlessly while others suffer from stress and failure in communication? The answer may lie in their emotional intelligence.

Emotional intelligence is the ability to manage and understand one's own emotions, as well as the emotions of others. One of my initial steps towards improving my own emotional intelligence was learning how to communicate effectively with others. This meant actively listening to others and allowing them to share their thoughts and feelings. I found that when I stopped talking and listened to others, I gained new perspectives and insights.

You must draw upon the knowledge and skills you have gained thus far and your ability to truly regulate your emotions to grasp the concept.

KEY CONCEPTS OF LISTENING

There are a few key concepts in listening that need to be addressed to be a good listener. They are the basics. One is active listening which means trying to understand what the person is saying. You can do this by making eye contact, nodding, and responding with something subtle. to show you're paying attention. Active listening leads to better communication and understanding.

Another is empathetic listening which is hearing and trying to understand their feelings and point of view. This can involve reflecting on their emotions, asking follow-up questions, and being patient and nonjudgmental. Empathetic listening can help build trust and a better connection with the person you're talking to.

Then there's critical listening. This means evaluating what someone is saying and figuring out whether it's accurate, relevant, and credible. This can involve considering the person's qualifications, checking the evidence they present, and looking for any flaws in their reasoning. Critical listening leads to more informed and rational decisions.

Understanding that all types of listening are important in different situations and for various purposes is essential. Using a combination of them can lead to greater communication.

TECHNIQUES FOR LISTENING

Being a good listener takes work. It's not just about hearing what someone says but understanding its meaning and responding correctly. By the end of this section, you'll have a solid understanding of what it takes to be a good listener and how to apply that in real-life situations.

Mirroring is a technique to show someone that you're listening to them and understand what they're saying. Repeat to them what they just said in your own words. This helps to confirm that you heard them correctly and can encourage them.

It's a great way to make the person feel heard and understood. It helps build trust and rapport between you and that person. So, try it next time you're in a conversation.

Paraphrasing is a technique that can help you become a better listener. It means restating what the person you are talking to is saying in your own words. This lets you understand their message better and lets them know you're following what they say. When you paraphrase, you're showing that you're actively listening and want to understand the person's message. It's important not to interrupt or change the message's meaning when you paraphrase but to restate it in a way that is easy for you to understand. It's also a good idea to check in with the speaker after paraphrasing to ensure you've understood their message correctly. You can improve your communication with others by using paraphrasing as a technique.

When you're having a conversation, one way to ensure you understand what the other person is saying is by asking questions. This is called the questioning technique. It's a way to get more information and clarify what the person is saying. It's important to ask open-ended questions that allow the person to fully express themselves, rather than closed-ended questions where only a yes or no is required. Asking questions shows that you're engaged in the conversation and genuinely interested in understanding. Plus, it leads to greater understanding between people. So next time you're in a discussion, ask some questions to understand better what the person is saying.

Summarizing is when you briefly repeat to the speaker the main points they've made. This helps confirm that you understood what they said and can keep the conversation on track, especially in group settings. It's a simple technique, but it can significantly affect how well you understand and retain information. Next time you're in a conversation, try summarizing what the other person said and see how it provides a greater understanding and rapport between you and them.

When it comes to nonverbal listening, it's all about paying attention to what people are saying without using words. This includes body language, facial expressions, and tone of voice. Awareness of these nonverbal cues is essential because they can give much information about a person's thinking or feeling. For example, if someone crosses their arms or avoids eye contact, they may feel defensive or closed off. On the other hand, if they're leaning in or making a lot of eye contact, they might feel open and engaged.

Nonverbal listening can also involve being aware of your body language and how it might affect the conversation. You can use nonverbal cues to show that you're paying attention and to build rapport with the person you're talking to.

Reading people's nonverbal cues can be challenging, but the more you pay attention, the better you'll get at it. And the more you know what someone thinks or feels, the better you can understand and communicate with them.

Reflective listening is a technique that involves reflecting on what the speaker has said, in your own words, to show that you understand their message. It's a simple yet powerful way to show that you're listening and caring about what the other person is saying.

By using reflective listening, you're showing that you understand the speaker and encouraging them to continue speaking. It's an excellent tool for building trust and rapport in any conversation. Use it to help improve and deepen your relationships.

Perspective-taking is a crucial technique to master. It's all about putting yourself in the other person's shoes and understanding where they're coming from. This means looking at things from their point of view and trying to understand their thoughts, emotions, and narratives.

It's also important to be aware of your biases and prejudices. Try to set them aside when perspective-taking. It may take some practice, but with time and effort, you'll be able to master this technique and become a more effective listener.

Feedback is when you tell someone exactly how you received their message. It can be positive or negative. It allows the speaker to adjust their message if they choose.

When giving feedback, it's essential to be specific and give examples which lets the speaker know how their message was received, and it will ensure clarity and understanding. It's important to be honest and respectful when giving feedback so that you will understand how you process information. Feedback is a powerful tool that can help you improve your communication with others.

Self-reflection is a powerful technique that can help you become a better listener. It's all about taking a step back and looking at yourself, your thoughts, and your actions. By doing this, you can identify any of your biases or assumptions affecting your listening so you can overcome them.

It's important, to be honest with yourself and to be willing to admit when you're wrong. By being aware of your biases, you can be a more objective listeners and better understand others. This technique benefits personal growth and self-awareness, leading to better relationships and communication. It's a simple but powerful tool that you can use to improve your skills.

When it comes to listening, one technique that can be helpful is called "pausing." Pausing is all about taking a moment to stop and think before responding to someone. This can help you make sure you understand what the other person is saying, and it can also help you avoid interrupting or reacting too quickly.

It's important to remember that pausing is not just about taking a physical break but also a mental break, allowing your mind to process the information and respond thoughtfully and accurately. By using the pausing technique, you'll be able to have more meaningful conversations and avoid misunderstandings. It's a simple technique, but it can make a big difference in your communication. So, next time you're in a conversation, try taking a brief pause before responding. You'll be surprised at how much more effective a listener you'll become.

The listening cycle is a technique that breaks down the process of listening into stages and can help you understand how you process information and become a better listener. The listening cycle includes receiving, understanding, evaluating, and responding to the other person.

In the receiving stage, you take in what the other person is saying. This is where you're listening and paying attention to them. Once you've received the information, you move on to the understanding stage. This is where you try to make sense of what the person is saying. This allows them to fix anything in their statement.

Next is the evaluating stage. This is where you decide if what the person is saying is accurate, important, or relevant.

Finally, you respond. This is where you give your input, whether the response is feedback or a response to the person's words.

Understanding the listening cycle helps you know how you listen and where to improve. It's a tool that can help you become a better listener and improve your communication with others.

NAME-DROPPING

Another practice that can help you gain a deeper understanding of others is remembering their name. Remembering people's names after they've been introduced to you is an effective communication tool, but if you're like I was, it's probably difficult for you to remember people's names.

This small act of remembering someone's name can make them feel more comfortable and valued, and it's also a great way to improve your memory. By repeating new information multiple times and practicing recalling it from memory, you can solidify the information in your brain for easier recall later.

If you struggle with remembering names, don't worry - it's a common issue. But with some practice, you can learn how to improve.

I first learned this quick lesson when I first interviewed for a head baseball coaching position. I met the personnel director right in front of the dugout on the practice field. We shook hands, and I said the obligatory "Hi, I'm Aaron," and he replied. But his reply was, "Nice to meet you, Aaron..." then he introduced himself. I gave him an odd look. He chuckled and said, "that helps me remember names. After someone says their name, I repeat it back immediately."

So, if you want to improve your ability to remember names, try repeating the person's name back to them immediately after they say it and then repeating it to yourself later in the conversation. And after the conversation, say their name to yourself one more time. You'll be surprised at how much better you'll get at remembering names with a bit of practice.

Listening is a crucial skill that can enhance your social, family, and professional relationships. The primary techniques include mirroring, paraphrasing, questioning, summarizing, nonverbal listening, reflective listening, perspective-taking, feedback, self-reflection, pausing, and listening for understanding. Additionally, we discussed the name-dropping memory technique for remembering people's names. These techniques can lead to positive outcomes in your relationships.

CHAPTER 12

In This Present Freedom

The new light and love you see in your reflection is a transformative experience, unlike anything you've felt before. You are taking ownership of your allegiances, identities, and emotions and placing them properly in your mind. This shift in perspective makes you the decision-maker, and it's time for action.

Please don't keep this change to yourself; share it with others and become a leader in your community. Your family and friends can learn from the new reflection in the mirror, and by sharing your experience, you can spread more love in any direction of your focus. Use your transformation to inspire and influence those around you. You are breaking out of your cycle; give them the tools to break out of theirs. You have no reason to be scared anymore. Be bold.

A VOICE CARRYING BEYOND THE TREES

Does the term "lead" scare you? First, you have the tools to deal with being scared now. You know where that fear comes from, and you know its name. The fear of leading is common and understandable. Most of that fear comes from the thought that you may fail. But go back to when you began understanding your emotions; you can handle anxiety now and move past fear.

Remember when you were younger, and you thought about what you wanted to be when you grew up? Do you know anyone that wanted to be "the boss" so they could tell everyone what to do or be in charge?

It's with that thought that one more time, I will let you use me as an example of someone who failed, then learned from the mistake to rise into a way of thinking.

My first dose of authentic leadership was also my first dose of the power of negativity in society. It was well before social media, which you see every day. We were lying on our packs; my team was not currently training. The other team, led by my friend Keegan, was doing their training on the rifle range.

Our radio operator was in the tall radio tower, watching the entire training ground. He was given to us by the battalion. He was not normally with us. Sergeant Morgan yelled to the radio tower to check on our "chow," that's what breakfast, lunch, and dinner are called in the Marine Corps.

The radio operator, a Private First Class, yells down that he's "getting to it" and to "hold on!" A Private First Class is about as low as it goes in the rank structure in the Marine Corps, with only privates and recruits below that. I, at the time, was a Lance Corporal, the rank that unofficially runs the Marine Corps. Before the radio operator could pronounce the "n" in "hold on!" I was seven steps up the stairs to the top of the tower. You have never seen someone climb a tower so fast.

Before the echo of his words had finished through the trees, I was one inch from his face, lighting him up with the intensity and adrenaline of the final light on a drag-racing light tree! It was electric! The firing line was in full training mode, and even they stopped to witness one of the most effective teardowns in recent memory.

This young radio operator was pale white and couldn't even say his name. He stuttered, stammered, and fought back the tears as I walked him through his entire life, from his "illegitimate" birth to his eventual lonely death.

Yes, I was that bad. But immediately after this, I was called down by our platoon sergeant, who immediately promoted me to team leader, which moved me from the second squad to the third squad with Keegan. One of the best things that ever happened to me was at that moment. Moving from second to third squad put me directly into the path of my friend Keegan.

The first thing he said to me was, "that was loud, but it's not how I would have done it," then he chuckled. Did you cringe when you read how I dealt with the radio operator? It's okay to cringe at that. I do now.

Years later, that conversation still echoes. I don't even think Keegan remembers it. But I do because it shifted me enough to deliver a thought, "was that wrong?" That's how I was always taught in the Marines. The loudest one in the room is the best leader, right? Yet, Keegan seemed to have a different philosophy.

Now that I was in Keegan's squad, we worked hand-in-hand as team leaders. We had a third team leader with us, but neither of us could remember who it was or even if they existed at all.

Keegan's leadership was strong, and my past bullying, though subsiding now, still had an impact, rendering the third team leader ineffective. It all came down to Keegan being such a strong leader that he completely changed my thinking with one phrase. "That's not how I would have done it!" What does that even mean? I would learn what that meant soon.

Though there are many effective leadership styles, I was firmly grasped by Keegan's leadership style because it was so effective and productive for us. Learning how to use Keegan's leadership style took me a while.

Still, eventually, it became an everyday practice for me. I was so ingrained in this new style that not long later, he and I stood together in the face of a court-martial while defending our entire platoon against an abusive tactic.

The same younger Marines I once abused and tormented with my attitude are now the ones on whom Keegan and I are wagering our futures.

Our leaders were attempting to bilk money from the Marines in our company. After forcing everyone to adhere to their demands, Keegan and I stood as the last two holdouts. We hoped that if we could fight and win, the rest of our platoon would win since he and I represented the lower chain of command.

Keegan and I were being threatened with "blackballing" if we did not adhere to their threats. They even came down to get Keegan and me to escort us for the reading of our rights.

They used the tactic of "fear" as their dominant leadership trait. The same fear tactic I used in the tower for that young radio operator. That same fear tactic I talked about earlier. That same fear tactic I had killed off - the same tactic that unfortunately rose again in me at the end of my first marriage.

This event taught me that effective leadership is not about being the loudest or most aggressive but about understanding and respecting the perspectives of others and finding common ground.

Keegan was called in for reading the rights first while I stood outside the office under supervision. Keegan argued so much with the command that a more calm, level-headed Captain had to take over the case from our two leaders and coordinate an amicable agreement between them and us.

Keegan walked out of that room, flashed his patented smirk, layered with extra confidence, and said, "we're good. Let's go!" I wasn't even required to testify or set foot in the room. Until he walked out of the room with a victory, he and I were going to face court-martial, and the threats against the other Marines would stand. We did it. He did it.

It took Keegan's leadership style in not just this instance but many more over the years to stand up in the face of a monster, have confidence in himself and have the ability to communicate effectively, to win. Along with Keegan, it also took that other Captain to step in front of our two leaders to communicate a reasonable agreement between everyone involved. It took leaders.

Though there are many different leadership styles, these two men found common ground to meet in agreement. Keegan would exhibit this effectiveness in his style often during our time in the Marine Corps.

That day we left those other two leaders with nothing more than their uniforms and empty words as their careers fizzled shortly after.

We weren't trying to destroy their careers. Those two "leaders" just weren't willing to recognize and adapt to what style was needed to be effective for our platoon.

It seemed to us that they only wanted to be the loudest ones in the room. It appeared they wanted fear to rule the day. It seemed they loved fear more than strategic and authentic leadership.

It's no wonder Keegan eventually became an officer and had a lasting career in the Marine Corps. His leadership changed my life. I do not doubt that he positively changed the lives of others.

He was an effective leader with emotional intelligence and an understanding of who he was. He is an unrivaled example of leadership in my life to this day.

SERVANT LEADERSHIP

Another principle of leadership is the "servant leader" principle. You need to understand the concept of servant leadership. This leadership style, first introduced by Robert K. Greenleaf many years ago, focuses on putting the needs of others first and serving the people you lead.

You have already learned in previous chapters about the importance of active listening and emotional intelligence in leadership. These skills are crucial in the practice of servant leadership. To truly serve those you lead, you must understand their needs and emotions.

One key aspect of servant leadership is empowering others. Giving your team members the tools and resources, they need to succeed enables them to take ownership of their work and make decisions for themselves. This improves their job satisfaction and engagement and allows them to contribute more effectively to the team and organization.

Another critical aspect is leading by example. As a servant leader, you must lead by the same principles and values that you expect from your team. This means being willing to take on the most difficult tasks, being open to feedback and criticism, and admitting when you are wrong.

Servant leadership can positively relate to organizational behavior and team effectiveness. Servant leaders tend to have more engaged and satisfied employees, leading to much higher productivity and performance in the workplace. By embracing servant leadership principles, you can improve your team's performance and create a more positive and fulfilling work environment for yourself and those around you.

I learned that authentic leadership involves listening, empathizing, and inspiring others to be their best selves. And it's about leading by example, not just by words. I also learned that authentic leadership is not about being perfect but about admitting when you're wrong and learning from your mistakes. It's about being humble enough to accept feedback and make changes when necessary. And it's about being compassionate and understanding, even when dealing with difficult situations or people.

The term "lead" may scare you, but it doesn't have to. With the right tools and mindset, anyone can become an effective leader. And it's never too late to learn and grow. Be willing to learn from the example of others and be open to new perspectives and ways of thinking. Though my voice carried beyond the trees from that tower, Keegan's has carried beyond it all with true power.

THE BEGINNING OF WAR

Leadership does not mean you are now in a position to cause people to suffer. You should be in a mindset where you want everyone around you to rise. I have had many great leadership examples in my life and many terrible examples of leadership in my life, but each of them had good and bad points. I do not throw away the entire person because of one action.

On that note, let's take a pop quiz to gauge your level of understanding of this journey. Remember the boss that had me fired for questioning his insult toward that woman? Over a decade after that situation, I walked into that same building for a quick meeting.

The person talking to me had been there for a long time; they were hired shortly after I was fired. So, I figured they would know about my former boss. I asked this person if my former boss was around so I could talk to him. The immediate reply was, "We fired him long ago. He was doing some bad things. He even got divorced because of it. Nobody knew he was a bad guy until it was too late." I was not shocked.

It took me a second to recover positive thoughts. This man tried to ruin my career, only to discover that I was proven correct over a decade later. This was a tough discovery for me because it reminded me of the suffering afterward. The unemployment and the damage caused by my former boss. He wrecked my family.

Leadership means striving for others' success, not causing suffering. A former boss who tried to ruin my career was later fired for the same reasons I brought up. It reminded me of the suffering he caused, including unemployment and damage to my family.

Reflect on how you would feel in my situation if your career and life were ruined by someone who was later fired for their actions. Answer the questions honestly before proceeding. How would you feel in my shoes and this situation was thrown in your lap?

Who are the characters in my story about my former boss? There is the owner, the executive, then me, the staffer. Who are the victims, and who are the victors?

Everyone suffered in the story. The owner lost two workers who, despite attitudes, were both productive and contributed to the flow of the company. The executive lost his job and his marriage and incurred embarrassment in front of many people to the point that he became a recluse. I lost my job and suffered similar embarrassment in front of many people, which forced me to rebuild my career from scratch when it was just beginning.

Who won in this story? Nobody won, did they? We all suffered because of the actions of others and the consequences of our choices, regardless of their merit. I presented an idea to the owner that the executive was causing damage to the company through his negative actions. The owner didn't listen to me. Instead, he fired me and kept the executive.

Later, the owner would discover that the executive was doing precisely what I said he was doing and subsequently fired him.

This story is why all of this teaching is so important. Relationships are messy, and the lines of war are always blurred.

The beginning of war is always in the self. If you need something to provide gain to "self," you will seek to acquire it. Beit was insulting others to elevate self. Beit was telling on a boss to look good to the owner. Beit was firing a squeaky wheel to avoid firing your executive.

War begins in the pursuit of "self" in the smallest form of tiny, insignificant differences and then crescendos into its largest form, which is only held by whatever force causes a border. So, I suppose our only border to war currently is the stratosphere.

SIDE-EFFECTS INCLUDE

You may have experienced the consequences of holding grudges and seeking revenge. But let me remind you from earlier lessons in this message that these negative emotions can harm your well-being more than you could ever imagine.

Holding grudges and seeking revenge can consume your thoughts and emotions, leaving you angry and bitter. This can destroy your peace and prevent you from enjoying life's simple pleasures.

Remember, focusing on negative thoughts and emotions can also lead to mental and emotional exhaustion. This can leave you feeling drained and unable to tackle life's challenges with any energy or level of positivity.

Furthermore, holding a grudge can cloud your judgment and prevent you from making good decisions. This can impact not only your personal life but also your professional life.

So, it's important to remember that holding grudges and seeking revenge can only bring temporary satisfaction. In the long run, they can harm your mental and emotional well-being and prevent you from living a happy and fulfilling life.

Instead, focus on letting go of the past and moving forward with love and forgiveness. This will help bring you true peace and end the cycle.

ARE YOU WEAK?

Facing and managing your suffering shows true toughness. You are capable of more than you know, and it's time to rise to this fight for your freedom, peace, and the end of your cycle.

Was I weak when I didn't want to keep suffering from seeing my best friend like that? Was I weak when I thought I had a chance to find that missing man? Was I weak? No, I faced suffering like you are now.

I made a choice. I woke up, decided to fight, and I won. I won a battle against a phenomenon that science can't fully define. That is not weak; that is beyond human. That is your path now. You are waking up to the most incredible fight of your life.

Ten telling you no,
Nine telling you to go.
Eight breaking your heart,
Seven tearing your dream apart.
Six stealing your light,
Five taking your sight.
Four taking your heart,
Three hating you from the start.
Two mock everything you do,
One is the same as you.
Then there is you, no crowd in your eyes.
You are the one ready to rise!

THESE THOUSANDS OF DAYS

Taking your life back only happens if you breathe life into others. I had to learn it's not about me; It's about you. Be transformed by the renewing of your mind and take every thought captive. You have seen how to do that; learn and practice these tools. You can master this, and you will find your "self" when you do; maybe you'll find me nearby. I never stopped looking for anyone that I lost. I looked for your son and your daughter; I looked for you.

> You again, familiar character,
> I'll play you one more time.
> The path ahead looked grim.

> All this time looking for someone,
> The first one was found, and all after that,
> In this brazen audacity to win.

Hundreds of spins in the cycle, these thousands of days. Every day it seemed as if someone who was loved and didn't know it took their life. I couldn't stop it; so, I could not define these thousands of days. I could never escape the reality that I was saved, and others were not. I lost my breath for a moment, but it returned so that I may breathe life into anyone. I was held up for a reason.

YOU ARE THAT REASON.

This is the door. You are at the door. I can't tell you what the handle looks like or how to open it; you have to do that. I had to move the camera back and take the remote. I took back my life from the liar. These thousands of days, and I see it today. I see my children's faces. I see the one who held me up from the drop, and I feel the breath. I feel the life. Breathe life!

No longer subject to that version of me in that chair. No longer subject to the one who is picking my life for me. I have freedom from the cycle that held me for these thousands of days. I have defined the ineffable. You have your chance at freedom and the breath of life. Find a way.

Define the ineffable.

Mom.
I beat the pain.
I found my breath.
In this melody is a song.
This melody is a kiss on my ear.
A bright light, The owner of life, At last.
The embrace, the warm current rushes me.
The final light, the joyful release that brings peace.
This is the one who turns on the final breaker.
It is the one; the name is too rich to speak.
The one who is with me through.
I see in a mirror dimly.
Soon, face to face.
In part, I know.
I am known.
I will know fully.
Clear face-to-face.
But for now, I see dimly.
The final breaker is being reset.
The breakers are all being returned.
Please. Let. Me. Rest. In. This. Present. Freedom.
That peace, the easing peace will never fade away.
White flashes dance through the rising light.
My face calms, great breath in my lungs.
The wisps cease and fade away.
The rising light.
RISE!

Acknowledgments

I will undoubtedly miss someone because that is just how these things work. So, I'll do this; I will go through my phone and emails and thank the last few people I talked to about this message. I'll add a few more here and there. I'm only going to add people I talked to directly about this writing or stories. Then, I will take the list to a randomizer and scramble it up. Fair enough? One exception, the family goes first.

Nancy Childress, Isaac Ja. Childress, RaeAnn Childress, Dana Childress, McKenzie Horsch, Isaac Jo. Childress, Brynlee Childress, Benjamin Childress, Don Wallen, Carolyn Wallen, Rachel Magnuson, Matt Magnuson, Alex Sturgess, Kathy Brier, Jeremy Brier, Justin DeShong, Kirby DeShong, Travis Smith, Matti Sicker, Jason Wohlgemuth, Keith Johnson, George Pardos, B. Wayne Barkley, Amber Chaib, Mike O'Connor, Josh Stephens, Mark Gould, Travis Hofer, Gabe Stecker, Steven Keegan, Adam Bird, Tankmachine, Mark Dennett, Vincent Vargas, De'Anthony Thomas, Grady Powell, Jed Speer, Paula Downs, Frank Garcia, Andy Skeels, Stephen Baldwin, Bobby Massey, Marcus Castillo, Andy Nepper, Henry Fontanills, Austin Strecker, Kim Nerstrom, Cade Armstrong, Richard Bradley, Don Bramer, John Fannin, Richard Hocutt, Nick Palmisciano, Santiago Hungria, Vaughn Neville, Troy Trussel, Lynette Herrman, John [redacted], and probably a ton more. Text me, and I'll make sure not to miss you in the next one!

ABOUT THE AUTHOR

AARON CHILDRESS

Aaron Childress has decades of experience in the mental health industry. He has a wealth of knowledge in public speaking, including keynote addresses, workshops, writing, acting, production, and media appearances.

He is known for his unique ability to incorporate motivational and inspirational elements into his presentations, making them tailored to the needs of the audience and event coordinators. He has a strong passion for self-discovery and personal development. Aaron, his wife, RaeAnn, and their family live in Wichita, Kansas.

For more information, go to:
aaronchildress.com/info

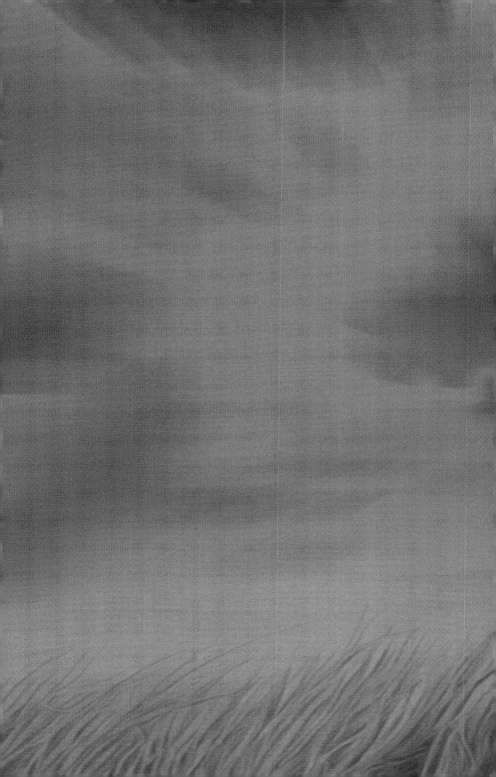

Another Field to Burn

One step has already been taken.
The healing is removing painful lines.
Remember how it slipped through the weeds,
One small step at a time.

One step has already been taken.
But the field can become bitter in time.
Soil becomes rotten, and parasites steal the fruit.
One small step can add a painful line.

Watch closely over this field.
Watch for the tares and the soil to turn.
If you miss them and they come in the night,
There will be another field to burn…

See you soon.

AC

Made in the USA
Columbia, SC
09 March 2024

32422871R00120